THERESE RAQUIN

THERESE RAQUIN

by Leslie Sands
based on the novel by Emile Zola

LONDON

A member of the Chappell and Intersong Music Group

First published 1985
by ETG, English Theatre Guild Ltd, 129 Park Street,
London W1Y 3FA.

© Copyright Leslie Sands 1985

ISBN 0 85676 026 9

Typeset and printed by Commercial Colour Press, London E7.
Cover design by Robin Lowry.

The play was first presented (under the title DEADLOCK) by Lyceum Productions Ltd., at the Poole Arts Centre, Dorset, on 1 April 1985, with the following cast.

THERESE	Hildegard Neil
LAURENT	Jack Carr
MADAME RAQUIN	Hazel Douglas
CAMILLE	David Plaut
GRIVET	Desmond Jordan
MICHAUD	Nicholas Smith

Directed by Knight Mantell

The play is set in Paris in the mid-1870's.

The action takes place in the living-room over a haberdasher's shop in the Pont Neuf district of Paris.

ACT I

Scene 1	An evening in September.
Scene 2	The following Sunday.

ACT II

Scene 1	Afternoon, a year later.
Scene 2	Midnight, six weeks later.

ACT III

Evening, some months later.

photo from the original production by Lyceum Productions Ltd.

ACT ONE

Scene One

The living-room has a lofty ceiling and is wallpapered in a faded and undistinguished grey. Up Right is an archway, through which may be glimpsed the hand-rail of a staircase, descending to the shop below; this area also gives access to MADAME RAQUIN'S *bedroom, which is understood to be off-Right. Up Left, and at an angle to the rest of the room, is a bedroom alcove, with bed and night-table or low shelves. Both arch and alcove may be fully screened off by curtains as and when necessary.*

The door to the small kitchen is in the Left Wall, and Down Left is the ornate fireplace. Facing this (Down Right) is a sash-window that looks out on the roofs of Paris. The bedroom alcove has windows also, and some of these have been converted to form a glass door that is normally kept locked and leads to a narrow outside stairway.

Down Right, a chaise longue; upstage in the Right Wall, built-in bookshelves; two armchairs near the fire, one green and one blue; in the middle of the Back Wall, a substantial sideboard or dresser; fairly centrally situated, a circular table with flaps (at present extended), covered with an oilcloth cover.

If space is available, other furnishings could include a tall cupboard used for clothes, a small work-table, a stool and numerous shelves, all crowded with shabby oddments. The general effect should be one of cluttered comfort, combined with practicality.

An evening in September.

The bedroom alcove is shut off by the curtains, and from behind them comes muffled laughter and the sounds of a lovers' struggle. THERESE RAQUIN *bursts through the curtains, her dress hastily flung on, the bodice still wide open. She is a lithe and beautiful animal, with a touch of the mulatto about her. A male arm, bare, extends from the alcove, trying to hold her back.*

THERESE	*(laughing, breathless)* No! Let me — go!
	She breaks free and, still laughing, runs to the mantel to check on a clock there. Then, hurrying, she comes downstage and starts to lace up her bodice as LAURENT *emerges through the curtains, lazily doing up his shirt and rolling down the sleeves.*
LAURENT	What's all the rush?
THERESE	Do you know what time it is?

LAURENT	No.
THERESE	It melts away when you're here.
LAURENT	I don't believe in clocks and watches, they're all illusions. This is the only reality; a man, a woman and — this.

He puts both arms around her waist and swings her round towards him.

THERESE	Are you never satisfied?
LAURENT	Never. (*Kisses her*) Neither are you. (*Kisses her again*) Admit it.
THERESE	(*pouting*) I still don't know why I let you come near me today. You didn't deserve to, keeping away for a whole week like that. What's the matter? Are you frightened I love you too much?
LAURENT	That's not possible.
THERESE	(*teasing*) Frightened we'll be caught, then? I've told you, as long as you use that door (*points to alcove*) and we're careful, it's quite safe. No-one's going to find out.
LAURENT	I'm scared the whole world's going to find out — that one day I'll go home shouting out loud in the streets how much I love you.

They embrace passionately, then he breaks from her and goes to the stairhead, where he stands listening.

THERESE	It's only the house; the damp makes the stairs creak.

She puts her foot up on a stool, the better to straighten her stockings and adjust her garters, her skirts held high. LAURENT crosses in admiringly.

LAURENT	That flesh of yours. It glows like alabaster in warm sunlight.
THERESE	You're supposed to be a painter, not a poet!
LAURENT	All artists appreciate beauty; they live by it. (*Strokes her leg*) Does Camille ever show his appreciation?

THERESE	(*slaps his hand*) Go away.
LAURENT	Over here, for instance, on this bed of ours?
	He drags back the curtains at the alcove. The bed is rumpled and his jacket lies across it. THERESE *is suddenly quieter.*
THERESE	Never. No.
LAURENT	I can't think what you ever saw in him.
THERESE	My aunt gave me a home when I was seven years old. Nobody else wanted me. Sometimes I think I married him out of gratitude.
LAURENT	What happened on your wedding night?
THERESE	That's not the sort of question you should —
LAURENT	(*masterfully*) I want to know. I have the right.
	Slight pause.
THERESE	We were married in Normandy. That night, we went up the stairs as usual; instead of going into my bedroom on the left, I went into Camille's on the right. And that was all.
LAURENT	It's the truth — you promise?
THERESE	(*winds her arms about him*) You're jealous! And there's no reason on earth. (*Presses into him*) I've never loved anyone as I love you — from the very first night he brought you here.
LAURENT	I didn't want to come; he had to force me.
THERESE	I was sitting near the fire, doing some embroidery, and secretly watching the pair of you. You didn't know, you were too wrapped up in your stupid game. Suddenly this feeling gusted over me. I didn't know it was love then, it seemed more like hate. After that, whenever you came here, my nerves were stretched to breaking-point. Yet when you were away, I found myself longing for the pain. Then we made love —
LAURENT	On *our* bed.

THERESE	(*simply*) I knew from that moment you were all I wanted.
LAURENT	My darling.
	They clasp each other again.
MME. RAQUIN	(*off*) Thérèse . . . Thérèse!
THERESE	There now, you've left it too long. Hurry!
	She moves swiftly to open the door in the alcove. LAURENT *whisks up his coat from the bed and slips out, grinning.* THERESE *locks the door behind him and straightens the bed hastily before drawing the alcove curtains.*
MME. RAQUIN	(*off*) Thérèse, where are you?
	Her aunt, MADAME RAQUIN, *ascends the stairs, breathing hard. She is sixty, and, though a sturdy and self-confident woman of peasant origins, moves more slowly than we might expect.*
THERESE	Sorry — I've been in the kitchen.
MME. RAQUIN	(*gratified*) Putting things straight, I might have guessed. Though how you can see to work in this light.
THERESE	What have you done with the lamp?
MME. RAQUIN	In the kitchen — didn't you see it? I always trim the wick before they come on Thursdays.
THERESE	So you do. (*She goes off to fetch it.*)
MME. RAQUIN	Otherwise, Doctor Grivet complains the only domino he can see is the double-six.
THERESE	(*off*) That man! He'll go to his grave complaining about something.
MME. RAQUIN	He's a good doctor, for all that.
THERESE	(*off*) Then why don't you take some of the medicines he gives you?
MME. RAQUIN	I don't need his pills and potions, they can't make me any younger. But his company, that's always welcome.
	THERESE *returns, with a lighted oil-lamp.*

THERESE	I can't think why; he only comes here for the dominoes.
MME. RAQUIN	And when he loses, what an uproar! (*Peers at clock*) Where's that son of mine got to?
THERESE	You asked him to call in at the wine-shop for something special, don't you remember?
MME. RAQUIN	It's only on the corner. That can't have taken him till now. I do hope he's well wrapped up, these September evenings can be treacherous.
THERESE	He looked like a cocoon when he went off this morning.
MME. RAQUIN	Paris is cold all the year round. It makes me long for my old home in the country. One day I'll go back there, before I turn into an icicle!

She moves about the room, helping THERESE *to tidy it.*

THERESE	You'll never get Camille to go with you.
MME. RAQUIN	No, he's a true Parisian at heart. All the boys at home used to be so jealous of his fine manners and his great ambition. And he won't always be a humble clerk on the railway, mark my words. One day he'll be in command, and you'll be going to soirées and fine receptions — you forgot the glasses.
THERESE	I'm sorry. (*She goes back into the kitchen.*)
MME. RAQUIN	Not that I blame you: it's not every night the Raquin family has champagne!

The shop-bell goes as THERESE *hurries back in with the family's best glasses.*

THERESE	Someone in the shop — I'll go.
CAMILLE	(*off*) It's only me!

Her husband CAMILLE *runs up the stairs, carrying two bottles of a fair champagne. He is light and slim, handsome in an effete way, and a weakling.*

MME. RAQUIN	Camille, my darling. (*As he kisses her*) Two bottles?

CAMILLE	There'll be six of us, don't forget. Here's your change.
	He gives her some coins, smirking. MADAME RAQUIN *counts the money.*
THERESE	(*pointedly*) Good evening, Camille.
CAMILLE	(*ignores her*) See? All I spent was six francs. (*Flourishes champagne*) Three francs a bottle!
MME. RAQUIN	Only three?
	CAMILLE *puts down the bottles to divest himself of his hat, coat and voluminous scarf.*
CAMILLE	I went all the way to the Boulevard St. Michel where I'd seen them marked down in a grocer's. That's as good as any vintage wine at eight francs.
MME. RAQUIN	Two bottles for six francs! (*Proudly, to* THERESE) Such a businessman.
CAMILLE	Haven't you got any cakes?
THERESE	They're waiting in the kitchen.
	Again she goes off, as CAMILLE *bears his precious bottles to the sideboard.*
CAMILLE	Everybody knows wine-merchants are a lot of frauds and swindlers; it's only the label that's different. Of course, you've got to know something about the stuff.
	THERESE *comes back with a dish of cakes.*
MME. RAQUIN	Give them to me. We'll have everything on the sideboard, on display. Now the plates.
	THERESE *goes to fetch them obediently.*
CAMILLE	These are all éclairs and ground-rice tarts. Where's my favourite coconut?
MME. RAQUIN	There'll be no coconut till that stomach of yours clears up.
CAMILLE	There's nothing wrong with it. I caught a chill in that broken-down old office —
MME. RAQUIN	It always gave you trouble, even as a child.

THERESE *returns with plates, and puts them on the table.*

MME. RAQUIN   On the sideboard, I said! Really, Thérèse — you're so absent-minded, lately.

THERESE *transfers them without comment, then goes to sit at the work-table and takes out her needlework.*

CAMILLE   (*views the array*) That's better.

MME. RAQUIN   They'll think we've come into money, won the Lottery or something! Oh dear, I do hope he doesn't forget to bring the picture, after all this.

CAMILLE   That's the whole reason he's coming. Besides, he never forgets anything.

MME. RAQUIN   Why didn't you fetch it home when it was finished?

CAMILLE   Laurent wanted to have it framed first. Perhaps it won't be ready.

MME. RAQUIN   Then all the champagne will be wasted.

THERESE   (*drily*) We can always put it by for Laurent to drink some other day.

MME. RAQUIN   It's not only for him.

CAMILLE   Behave yourself, Thérèse. (*To his mother*) She's never liked any of my friends, all the years we've been here.

THERESE   He's the worst of the lot. Here every week, eating our food and guzzling our wine —

CAMILLE   You don't pay out for it, do you?

MME. RAQUIN   Besides, it's the only decent meal he gets. I feel sorry for him, perched up in that miserable attic and eating in workmen's cafés all the time.

CAMILLE   You should see it, Mama — the studio, I mean. I call it the Igloo. Of course, he can't afford any heating.

MME. RAQUIN   You should have told me; the poor boy could have done the picture here.

CAMILLE   The light wouldn't have been right. By the way, I've had a marvellous thought. To pay him back, we'll all go on a picnic this weekend — to Suresnes.

MME. RAQUIN   Suresnes! With all those noisy roundabouts? My nerves couldn't stand it. You children go — Laurent deserves a treat.

CAMILLE   (*doubtfully*) I'm not sure I want Thérèse there, if you're not coming. Do you know what she did last time? Wouldn't go on anything. Just sat on the ground, bolt upright, staring down at the water like a dreary old crow. We'd be better off by ourselves.

The shop-bell goes.

CAMILLE   Here he comes!

LAURENT *runs up the stairs with a framed portrait of* CAMILLE, *done up in rough sacking.* THERESE *studiously ignores him.*

LAURENT   Am I the first?

CAMILLE   Aren't you always?

MME. RAQUIN   The others won't be here till eight o'clock.

LAURENT   Good! I wanted you three to have a private view. (*Unwraps picture*) There — what do you think?

CAMILLE   Look, Mama — isn't it clever? Isn't *he* clever?

LAURENT *holds the picture in front of his chest. It is quite a presentable work.*

MME. RAQUIN   But it's so lifelike!

CAMILLE   (*bubbling*) Look at my dress suit: the cloth of that collar looks absolutely real.

MME. RAQUIN   So does the arm of the chair.

CAMILLE   Laurent painted it green, so it would look like that one. (*Points at his armchair*) The one we brought from Vernon.

LAURENT   You're not disappointed, madame?

MME. RAQUIN	I think it's absolutely splendid. And we must hang it up before they come, in the place of honour.
LAURENT	(*flattered*) Where?
MME. RAQUIN	Over the fire, of course. Camille, can you take that old landscape down?
LAURENT	I'll do it — if you're sure you want it there?
CAMILLE	It's the only possible place for it. Don't you think so, Thérèse?
THERESE	Does it matter what I think?
CAMILLE	I've warned you once tonight.
	The shop-bell goes.
MME. RAQUIN	No peace for the wicked. (*Moves to answer it*) It's not eight o'clock yet, it must be a customer. Someone wanting fresh ribbons for the weekend, I shouldn't wonder.
CAMILLE	Or a new hat.
MME. RAQUIN	Oh, I hope not. Hats always take so long…
	She goes off down the stairs. LAURENT *has taken down the landscape and looks round for somewhere to put it.*
THERESE	Over there, I'll see to it later.
CAMILLE	Laurent, look! (*Points at bottles*) We're celebrating.
LAURENT	Champagne!
CAMILLE	(*nods excitedly*) And that's not all. On Sunday, when I'm free of that wretched office, the three of us are going off on a picnic to Suresnes!
LAURENT	Better and better.
CAMILLE	Mama won't come, she likes to rest her legs on her day off.
THERESE	I don't have to come either if you'd rather be by yourselves.
LAURENT	I wouldn't hear of it. Would you, Camille?
CAMILLE	Of course she'll come. (*To his wife*) If you don't, who's going to see to the food?

LAURENT	Listen, I know somewhere better than Suresnes. It's always so crowded at the weekends — and the smell! What about St. Ouen? We can spend the afternoon out on the island and then have dinner at one of those little inns by the river. What do you say?
CAMILLE	I'll be sorry to miss the roundabouts.
LAURENT	They always make you sick anyway. And we won't have to dress up as much. Thérèse?
THERESE	We'll go wherever Camille wants.
LAURENT	There speaks a dutiful wife.
THERESE	No. It's just that he always gets his own way in the long run. (*She returns to her work.*)
CAMILLE	It's Laurent's idea, and I think its wonderful. St. Ouen it is!
THERESE	If you say so.
CAMILLE	I do! And I just hope you're not going to sit there like a stuck pig all evening. (*As she regards him darkly*) Look at those eyes, Laurent. When she was small, when Captain Degans left her with us, those great big staring eyes used to frighten me to death. They still can!
THERESE	Don't be so ridiculous.
CAMILLE	They say her mother was the daughter of an African chief — and her father was a renegade sea-captain. What a combination, eh?
LAURENT	He's only teasing.
CAMILLE	Of course I am. We all know she's a good girl at heart. (*Kisses her perfunctorily*) And I'll say this for her, she looks after me marvellously when I'm ill.
	MADAME RAQUIN's *voice comes from below.*
MME. RAQUIN	(*off*) Camille, come and do the shutters for me, will you?
CAMILLE	Coming. (*Crosses to stairs*) Laurent, will you give me a hand with the extra chairs?

LAURENT	(*indicates portrait*) As soon as I've done this.
	CAMILLE *potters down to join his mother, as* LAURENT *hangs the picture.* THERESE *comes to his side to admire it, her manner changing completely.*
THERESE	You've caught him exactly. It's Camille to the life.
LAURENT	It looks good up there.
THERESE	It could look better.
LAURENT	How?
THERESE	If that were you looking down on us instead of him.
LAURENT	Master of the house?
THERESE	You were made for it.
LAURENT	(*takes her hands*) If only you were free!
THERESE	Don't let me dream. The best dreams never come true.
LAURENT	This one might. When Camille comes back, just watch and listen.
THERESE	Laurent — you've thought of a way?
LAURENT	Watch. Listen. And wait till Sunday.
CAMILLE	(*shouts, off*) Laurent, what are you doing up there?
LAURENT	(*calls back*) Making love to your wife.
CAMILLE	(*off*) Oh, that's all right. But don't let Mama catch you at it!
LAURENT	Thérèse, how much would you dare?
THERESE	For us? Anything.
	CAMILLE *puffs his way upstairs, carrying two chairs.*
CAMILLE	I've done it myself, just to shame you both. But I shouldn't have — all this lifting's bad for the heart.
LAURENT	They're not heavy. (*He swings them easily into place at the table.*)
THERESE	You'd better sit down, Camille.

LAURENT	Yes, sit down — save your strength for Sunday.
CAMILLE	Sunday?
LAURENT	We're taking a boat out on the river and you can do most of the rowing.
CAMILLE	(*worried*) I'm not very good at it.
THERESE	The Seine? His mother would never allow it.
CAMILLE	You mind your own business. Nobody tells me what to do and what not to do.
THERESE	You know what she'd say.
CAMILLE	If I want to go on the river I'll go on the river, whether she likes it or not.
LAURENT	Perhaps it's not such a good idea after all.
CAMILLE	She's only being awkward because you suggested it.
THERESE	What if we had an accident?
LAURENT	(*innocently*) They happen anywhere, don't they?
CAMILLE	Of course. In town, in the country, on the river and on dry land.
LAURENT	(*playing up*) Even in the street, a tile can fall off a roof and knock your brains out.
CAMILLE	And almost anyone can be struck by lightning!

The two friends laugh together like schoolboys.

THERESE	Very well. But only if you tell her first.
CAMILLE	I'll do as I please.
THERESE	If you don't, I shall.

He glowers at her. Outside, a clock starts to strike the hour.

LAURENT	Eight o'clock already? It can't be.
CAMILLE	(*counts aloud*) . . . five . . . six . . . seven . . . *eight.*

He points dramatically towards the stairs. DOCTOR GRIVET *is ascending them, with* MADAME RAQUIN *on his arm.*

MME. RAQUIN	Here's my doctor, on the dot as usual.

LAURENT	Good evening, Grivet.
GRIVET	Easy up the stairs, we have to watch those arteries of yours.
MME. RAQUIN	There he goes, making work for himself as soon as he arrives.
	They come into the room, GRIVET *is a dry old stick, fussy and garrulous.*
GRIVET	Good evening.
CAMILLE	Hello, doctor.
THERESE	Let me take your umbrella. (*She relieves him of it and and crosses with it to the fireplace.*)
CAMILLE	Not raining, is it?
GRIVET	I never trust anything about September, especially the weather. Excuse me, not that corner. (*He moves to the fire and positions the umbrella to suit himself.*) That's not the place for my umbrella. My umbrella goes in this corner.
MME. RAQUIN	Thérèse, take his goloshes.
GRIVET	Thank you, I can manage them myself. (*Sits, to do so*) I always do things for myself and then I know they're done properly. There. (*He slips them off and sets them beside the immaculately furled umbrella.*)
MME. RAQUIN	You're out of breath, doctor — it's most unlike you.
GRIVET	I'm not surprised. I was forced to hurry, otherwise I'd have been late.
CAMILLE	You're never late!
GRIVET	There was the most enormous crowd in the Rue St. André-des-Arts. I had to cross over, and that always upsets me. I keep to the left all the time and then I know where I am. Keep to the left, just like the trains.
MME. RAQUIN	What was everyone doing there?
GRIVET	I haven't the slightest idea.
LAURENT	Perhaps there's been an accident.

GRIVET	More than likely. Everyone goes at such a speed you take your life in your hands these days. (*He crosses and sits in front of the table.*) I'm not too sure I haven't pulled a muscle. Ah, it's good to sit down.
	A jovial voice booms out from the foot of the stairs.
MICHAUD	Good evening, everyone! I haven't kept you waiting, have I?
MME. RAQUIN	(*calls, happily*) Come up, monsieur.
	HENRI MICHAUD *comes into view, grunting with effort as he climbs the stairs. He is elderly, bushy-haired, and a burly ex-policeman.*
MICHAUD	Why you can't have your living-room on the ground floor like any other decent, law-abiding family — hello, I must be late. Grivet's got his watch out.
GRIVET	(*primly*) No more than usual. Your weekly average is four and a half minutes.
MICHAUD	One of these days I'm going to be here on time, just for the pleasure of giving you a stroke. My dear Madame Raquin. (*He sweeps his hat off and kisses her hand in old-world, courtly fashion.*) Anyway, I've got a perfect excuse this evening. Didn't any of you spot the excitement down the road?
GRIVET	I've just been telling everyone, it almost made me late. Most distressing.
MICHAUD	(*shaking his head*) A tragedy.
GRIVET	(*blinks*) My being late?
MICHAUD	No, you fool — the reason for the disturbance.
GRIVET	An accident of some sort?
MICHAUD	Worse, much worse.
GRIVET	I crossed over. It was nothing to do with me, and. . .
MICHAUD	Murder has to do with all of us, Doctor Grivet.
THERESE	Murder?

MICHAUD	(*nods*) They found a woman's body at the Hotel Viking. Cut into four pieces. In a trunk belonging to a guest who went off in the night. Worse still, the head was missing.
CAMILLE	How ghastly.
GRIVET	And I passed the place. I might have been murdered myself.
MICHAUD	No such luck.
GRIVET	I beg your pardon?
MICHAUD	(*smoothly*) Not with all those people about, I do assure you.
LAURENT	Have they caught the murderer?
MICHAUD	Unfortunately, no. The Inspector in charge, one of my old colleagues, as a matter of fact, says the police are baffled. The occupant of the room gave false particulars and has disappeared as mysteriously as he came.
MME. RAQUIN	Do they know who the poor girl was?
MICHAUD	Arms and legs are notoriously difficult to identify, madame; it's the head that adds distinction. Furthermore, the lady in question was completely naked.
CAMILLE	Naked and hacked to pieces —
GRIVET	Well, it's probably no-one we know. And murder is a fact of life in Paris these days. When Michaud was a superintendent of police, he had some grisly stories, I can tell you. (*To* MICHAUD) Remember the one about the gendarme who was buried in little bits? They found his fingers in a box of carrots. Do tell them.
MICHAUD	You've just told them for me.
MME. RAQUIN	Do let's talk of something else. All this about death and violence, you're making me shudder.
GRIVET	Don't worry, madame, you're quite safe here.
MICHAUD	Indeed you are. (*Crosses to fire*) This is what I'd call a God-fearing household; one of the very

few left in Paris. (*Looking around*) And it's looking rather special tonight. Champagne! Are we in for a celebration?

CAMILLE   It's in honour of my picture — just behind you.

MICHAUD turns and takes it in.

MICHAUD   Well, well, well — what's all this?

GRIVET   (*rises*) A portrait of Camille, I can see that from here. I keep telling you, you need glasses.

MICHAUD   What a splendid likeness! I can almost smell the flower in your buttonhole.

All gather round the picture with the exception of THERESE.

GRIVET   Now that's what I call a portrait. I can't stand this Impressionist stuff that's all the rage. It's nothing but a lot of coloured dots — anyone can *stipple* a picture.

MME. RAQUIN   Laurent finished it yesterday and had it framed today, as a present to my son.

MICHAUD   It shows considerable talent, young man, you have quite a future.

LAURENT   (*modestly*) Thank you.

CAMILLE   So the verdict's unanimous. Now we can have some tea.

MME. RAQUIN   What about the champagne?

CAMILLE   We'll drink to the picture after the dominoes. I like to keep a clear head for the game.

MME. RAQUIN   Whatever you say, Camille. (*Crosses to kitchen*) It won't take long. (*She goes off, as CAMILLE reaches for the two bottles.*)

CAMILLE   Actually, I want these to sit in a bucket of cold water for an hour or so. I like my champagne properly chilled. One must keep up one's standards. (*He goes off after his mother.*)

MICHAUD fills his pipe as GRIVET sits again at the table and polishes his pince-nez.

GRIVET	Quarter-past eight. That gives us plenty of time for the Conqueror.
LAURENT	Monsieur Michaud —
MICHAUD	Laurent?
LAURENT	Do a lot of criminals go unpunished nowadays?
MICHAUD	Ever since I retired, yes. (*He lights his pipe.*)
GRIVET	Disappearances... lingering deaths through starvation... fatal falls... not a cry heard, not a drop of blood spilt. In many cases the police seem powerless to act.
MICHAUD	That's not always their fault. They're a highly skilled and dedicated body of men. But when you've got nothing to go on... (*He spreads his hands.*)
LAURENT	What you're saying is, there could be more than one murderer walking the streets now, in broad daylight?
MICHAUD	No doubt about it. Where no blame attaches, there's often no shadow of suspicion.
GRIVET	It makes you laugh, doesn't it? When you think of the taxes we pay?
MICHAUD	I never laugh at my taxes, monsieur.
GRIVET	(*throughly enjoying himself*) Thugs and killers... cold-blooded assassins... strolling round as free as the breeze and never arrested,
THERESE	(*strained*) I wish you'd change the subject, I shan't sleep tonight.
LAURENT	Don't worry, he's only leading us on.
MICHAUD	Indeed I'm not. You, I, any one of us, could shake hands with a murderer tomorrow and never suspect it.
THERESE	That's a horrible thought.
LAURENT	There's no proof. How can he know what he confesses no-one knows?
THERESE	That's true. (*Staring at* LAURENT, *on a thought*) What no-one knows simply doesn't exist.

LAURENT   Exactly.

              A beat.

GRIVET   All I know is, if that tea doesn't hurry up, our
              dominoes may never exist!

THERESE   I'll see what I can do. (*She moves off gratefully to
              the kitchen.*)

LAURENT   And how long were you a detective, sir?

MICHAUD   Twenty years — but I was a policeman a lot
              longer than that. I started out as the lowest form
              of animal life, a humble gendarme in
              Normandy.

GRIVET   Which is where he met the Raquins.

MICHAUD   Madame used to let me shelter in her shop when
              it was raining, and there was always a cup of
              her special coffee and coconut cake to help pass
              the time.

GRIVET   He knew her long before she met her husband.

MICHAUD   And courted her, what's more! But then along
              came the dashing Jean-Pierre from Paris and he
              soon saw me off the premises!

              MADAME RAQUIN *comes back with tea-things.*

MME. RAQUIN   What are talking about now?

MICHAUD   Still crime, madame, of one sort and another.

MME. RAQUIN   Well, I'd like you to give it a rest. There are
              other things in life.

GRIVET   Such as dominoes. Now, how are we playing?
              Last week it was Camille and I against you and
              madame.

MICHAUD   Then this week we must change partners.

MME. RAQUIN   (*pours tea*) All right. But don't keep telling me
              what to do, doctor. I have a mind of my own,
              don't forget.

GRIVET   And a very shrewd one, madame, where
              business is concerned. Unfortunately, its acumen
              doesn't extend to the ivory pieces.

MME. RAQUIN   (*retorts*) You can't make a living out of dominoes. Anyway, I only play to make up a foursome.

All settle into their respective places.

GRIVET   Oh, that wretched pipe! I do wish you wouldn't smoke while I'm trying to concentrate. It's worse than the Long Bar at the Moulin Rouge.

MICHAUD   (*puffing away heartily*) Not that you've ever been there, doctor — or have you? (*Teasing him*) Part of your secret life, is it?

GRIVET   T'ch! I'd better have a cigar to kill the fumes.

He lights one up as MADAME RAQUIN *hands him and* MICHAUD *their tea.* CAMILLE *comes back from the kitchen, rubbing his hands together importantly.*

CAMILLE   All ready? (*He goes to the sideboard to take an expensive box of ivory dominoes out of the top drawer.*)

MME. RAQUIN   Will you take tea, my darling?

CAMILLE   No, thank you. I'm saving myself for the champagne. (*He brings the dominoes and sits in his green armchair behind the table ruling the roost.*)

MME. RAQUIN   Sugar, Doctor Grivet?

GRIVET   Just four lumps. May I? (*He helps himself.*)

MME. RAQUIN   Thérèse, look after Laurent.

THERESE *has no tea herself, but pours a cup and takes it to* LAURENT *at the fire, where he lounges against the mantelpiece, smoking a cheap cheroot.*

GRIVET   Well, isn't this delightful? Do you know, every Thursday morning when I open my eyes, I say to myself, 'Hooray! Tonight I'm going to play dominoes at the Raquins.'

MICHAUD   And since we've been doing it for years, do you ever take yourself completely by surprise?

MME. RAQUIN   All supplied? Then let's begin.

She nods at CAMILLE *who opens the box ceremoniously.*

CAMILLE	Ladies and gentlemen — the pieces! (*He empties them neatly on the table.*) And may the best man win.
GRIVET	Shuffle them well.
CAMILLE	(*doing so*) Naturally. Laurent, come and stand by me — bring me luck.
LAURENT	With pleasure. (*He saunters to* CAMILLE's *shoulder.*)
GRIVET	Now we each take seven —
MICHAUD	As domino-players will, to the end of time.
CAMILLE	I've got the double-six. That means I lead.
LAURENT	Splendid.
CAMILLE	It doesn't always pay.
LAURENT	What I mean is, who better than you, Camille, to be the first to go?

He smiles blandly at THERESE *who bends assiduously over her work.*

CURTAIN

Scene Two

The following Sunday evening. The table is clear, except for a snowy-white cloth, two soup-dishes and two spoons. There is a vase of Autumn flowers in the centre. MADAME RAQUIN *comes from the kitchen with bread on a breadboard and a large kitchen knife. She places these on the table and then crosses painfully to peer at the clock on the mantelpiece.*

MME. RAQUIN	(*mutters*) Half past ten! (*She glances up at the portrait.*) I'll make you dance, young man, for staying out till this hour. (*She moves towards her chair but pauses before sitting in it.*) Oh, these old legs of mine; they're like lead tonight, Camille.

The jangle of the shop-bell comes from below.

MICHAUD	(*off*) Don't trouble yourself, madame, it's only old Michaud.

She settles in her chair with a sigh of relief as he puffs his way up the stairs.

MME. RAQUIN   This is a fine time of night to call — and on a
              Sunday, too.

MICHAUD   The better the day, the better the deed.

              *He removes his hat and stands looking at her, clearly
              not at his ease.*

MME. RAQUIN   Well, sit down, now you're here. Can I offer
              you some soup?

MICHAUD   I don't think...

MME. RAQUIN   I have it ready for the children.

MICHAUD   No, thank you. But I wouldn't refuse a drink.

MME. RAQUIN   We don't keep any in the house, except when
              we have guests.

MICHAUD   I'm a guest —

MME. RAQUIN   An unexpected one.

MICHAUD   Then it's a good thing I came prepared.

              *He takes out a pocket-flask and sets it on the table.
              Then he simply gazes at it and seems at a loss for
              words.*

MME. RAQUIN   The usual procedure is to remove the cap and
              pour a small quantity into a glass...

MICHAUD   Suddenly I don't feel like it. (*He wanders away to
              hang up his hat and she regards him with some
              amusement. He catches her at it.*)

MME. RAQUIN   Something's troubling you?

MICHAUD   Profoundly.

MME. RAQUIN   What can an old friend do to help?

MICHAUD   Sit there, quite calmly, and hear me out.

MME. RAQUIN   (*clasps her hands*) What have you been up to now?

MICHAUD   It's not me, madame. I'd best come straight to
              the point. It's your son, I'm afraid.

MME. RAQUIN   Afraid?

MICHAUD   You know they all went on the river this
              evening?

MME. RAQUIN	Yes, and I wish they hadn't. These evening mists — so bad for his chest.
MICHAUD	The fact is, Camille's not back yet. The other two are downstairs. They called at my house first.
MME. RAQUIN	(*sobering*) Why should they do that?
MICHAUD	They wanted me to have a word with you before you see them. It seems there's been some sort of accident. The boat capsized.
MME. RAQUIN	And Camille got a soaking? My poor boy, where is he now?
MICHAUD	(*obliquely*) Thérèse and Laurent are back —they're safe.
MME. RAQUIN	Stop beating about the bush. Where's my son?
MICHAUD	We're — not sure, madame.

She utters a sharp cry and comes to her feet, clinging awkwardly to her chair. He pours cognac from the flask.

MICHAUD	Drink it, please.
MME. RAQUIN	No, no, I —
MICHAUD	Drink it and sit down. *Please*, madame.

She sips from it briefly and then turns away as he recaps the flask.

MME. RAQUIN	Where's Camille, what have they done with him?
MICHAUD	I'm going directly to St. Ouen.
MME. RAQUIN	My son...

She moves across to the portrait with her back to him. MICHAUD *goes to the stairs and calls down softly.*

MICHAUD	You can come up, now.

His eyes are still on MADAME RAQUIN, *troubled, as* LAURENT *ascends the stairs. He is in a borrowed outfit and carries a bundle of sopping clothes.*

LAURENT	I'm so very sorry, madame.

MADAME RAQUIN *makes no move or answer.*

MICHAUD	Where's Thérèse?
LAURENT	Gone to get you a carriage.
MME. RAQUIN	(*stonily*) How could you come back and leave Camille?

LAURENT glances at MICHAUD.

LAURENT	Leave him?
MME. RAQUIN	You should have stayed till he was found. It was heartless of you.
LAURENT	(*stammers*) Michaud — haven't you told her?
MICHAUD	I've told her he's missing. That's all we know for certain. Well, isn't it?

THERESE runs up the stairs, white-faced, wearing borrowed clothes.

THERESE	The man's waiting. He says he has the fastest horse in Paris.
MICHAUD	Thank you, my dear. (*Gets his hat*) I'll come back as soon as I can. Thérèse, see she gets some rest.

He bustles out and leaves them. They watch the old lady for a moment before LAURENT goes closer.

LAURENT	It's all my fault, madame. I'll never forgive myself.

There is no reply. THERESE crosses him and touches her aunt tenderly.

THERESE	You mustn't make yourself ill.

Finally, MADAME RAQUIN turns to face them. From somewhere, she has found a new strength.

MME. RAQUIN	Michaud will find him soon enough. He's never let me down in his life. Those aren't your clothes.
THERESE	The people at the inn, they found us something. (*Takes bundle from LAURENT*) These are ours.
MME. RAQUIN	They're sopping wet.

She takes the bundle off into the kitchen, closing the door behind her.

THERESE   She's taking it better than I thought.

LAURENT   It's that fool Michaud. He's given her reason to
             hope —damn him for not being man enough to
             tell the truth.

THERESE   Step by step, he said. We don't want an invalid
             on our hands.

LAURENT   Camille's gone for good. The sooner she realises
             that —

THERESE   (snaps) You tell her, then. Camille's dead.
             That's all you have to say — dead. Drowned.

             *He stares at her, biting his lip. Then he feels for a
             chair.*

LAURENT   My God, Thérèse, when you say it like that —

THERESE   We did it because it had to be done.

LAURENT   You weren't the one — the one who... (*He gives
             way, and starts to shake.*)

THERESE   I would have been, if I'd had your strength.
             That's what we both have to depend on now —
             your strength.

LAURENT   He fought like a wild beast — bit me on the
             neck. (*He shows her the wound, which is still
             bleeding.*)

THERESE   It's only on the surface, that'll soon heal. (*She
             takes out a lace handkerchief to wipe it clean.*)

LAURENT   When you do something like this; when you
             force yourself to —

THERESE   She'll hear you.

LAURENT   It's different from all the talking. My God, it's
             different. (*He clutches at her.*)

THERESE   Control yourself. She's clever, she could guess
             the truth. It all depends on what we tell her —
             and how we tell it.

             LAURENT *comes to his feet.*

LAURENT   You still love me, now it's over?

THERESE   More than ever. It makes the two of us one.

He touches her features, his hand trembling. The kitchen door opens and he leaves her, pulling up the workman's scarf about his neck to hide his wound. At the fire, he gazes up at CAMILLE. MADAME RAQUIN *comes in with a bowl of steaming soup. She crosses to the table and ladles it into the dishes.*

MME. RAQUIN   You must both eat. At a time like this, it helps.

THERESE   Yes. (*She sits to start on her soup.*)

MME. RAQUIN   Laurent, come and have yours.

LAURENT   Not without Camille.

MME. RAQUIN   He won't be away long. I've saved him the lion's share.

She goes to the alcove for two dressing-gowns and puts one carefully round THERESE's *shoulders.*

THERESE   (*quietly*) Thank you.

MME. RAQUIN   Laurent, you can use Camille's till he gets back.

She crosses with it, but he prevents her.

LAURENT   You still don't understand, madame. The currents in the river — they're strong and fierce.

THERESE   We all know he couldn't swim.

MME. RAQUIN   I wanted him to, but he was always afraid to learn.

THERESE   (*standing*) He's gone. We have to face it.

MME. RAQUIN   (*harshly, the composure breaking*) How can you give up so easily?

LAURENT   He couldn't be found, madame. He went under and — he couldn't be found. The currents...

MADAME RAQUIN *drags herself to her armchair and sits, trying to regain her composure.*

MME. RAQUIN   I want you to tell me every detail.

Pause. Then LAURENT *starts on his prepared story.*

LAURENT   We ordered dinner in the restaurant and then decided to go out in the boat again while it was cooking. Camille was at the tiller and I was rowing. He wasn't watching the course, trailing his hands in the water, laughing and joking. I warned him we were coming to a dangerous bit — it's where they set the eel-nets — but he wouldn't take any notice. Then we hit one of those thick stakes they use for fixing the lanyards. I felt the bump. The rope shot from his hands. Camille stood up in a panic and the boat went over. I . . .

He breaks off and sits, apparently overcome. THERESE *takes up the story.*

THERESE I was fighting for breath, half-drowned myself. Then Laurent put a fist under my chin and swam for the shore, holding me up. He saved my life.

Pause.

LAURENT As I dived in again I heard a shout from downstream. Then there was silence.

THERESE It was growing dark. Three times he went back in at different points — three times! He fought the currents till he could do no more. When I made him come out, there was blood on his mouth. Look.

She produces the handkerchief and shows the old lady the stains.

LAURENT He's been taken from us, madame. We'll never see him again.

MADAME RAQUIN *rises, staring about her wildly. Then she makes for her room.*

THERESE (*bars the way*) Where are you going?

MME. RAQUIN To get my shawl. To go and find him.

LAURENT It's no use —

MME. RAQUIN I'll search every inch of the river. I'll help Michaud —

She starts out again, but THERESE *grips her firmly by the shoulders.*

THERESE	He hasn't gone to find Camille; only to recover a dead body.

MADAME RAQUIN *swings round and gazes at her for a long moment. Finally she drops her head.*

MME. RAQUIN	I can't give up hope. Not till I see him. Forgive me. I'm an old woman. Stupid. Useless. But I'm also a mother. I've guarded and protected him for thirty years. Tonight, when he needed me most, I wasn't there.

THERESE *starts to guide her out.*

THERESE	Come to your room.
MME. RAQUIN	There'll be no rest —
THERESE	Lie down, at least.

MADAME RAQUIN *tries to resist but the attempt is only half-hearted. Then she starts to cry.*

MME. RAQUIN	Oh, Thérèse, I warned him — warned you all! That hateful river...

Weeping she allows herself to be led off. Alone, LAURENT *wipes his face slowly with his hands, still sweating after the ordeal. Then he feels eyes upon him, and turns slowly to face the portrait. He backs from it a pace. Trying to collect himself, he crosses to the sideboard and drags open the door of a low cupboard where wine is sometimes kept. He finds a bottle, but it turns out to be empty. He flings it into a chair nearby and searches feverishly, but without success. At last he slams the door shut and turns for the kitchen... only to find himself staring at the picture again, as though hypnotised.* THERESE *returns.*

THERESE	She won't go to bed. She's sitting in a chair by the open window, saying his name over and over.
LAURENT	I'm sorry for her. None of it was her fault.
THERESE	She made me marry him.
LAURENT	That's cruel, Thérèse.
THERESE	(*ignores this*) She wants you to stay the night.

Slight pause.

LAURENT   Is that what you want too?

THERESE   No. Someone has to be with her; and Michaud will be coming back.

LAURENT   Than shouldn't I be here?

THERESE   It's better if you're not.

                  LAURENT *nods, and turns from her. Again, he is looking at the picture.*

LAURENT   It's changed.

THERESE   How could it?

LAURENT   That's not the Camille I painted. Not that smile. And never those eyes. (*Shudders*).

THERESE   Put it out of your mind. Come back in the morning for your clothes. She'd like you to open up the shop.

LAURENT   *Tomorrow* — ? She's opening tomorrow?

THERESE   Everything must go on as usual. That's what she insists.

LAURENT   Why does she want me...

THERESE   (*suddenly strident*) We can't manage the shutters — Camille always did them for her!

                  A beat.

LAURENT   I'll be here at nine.

                  He goes straight out.

CURTAIN

ACT TWO

Scene One

Afternoon, a year later.

The room is tidy and spotlessly clean. The table has been moved under the window Down Right and the chaise longue now shares the Centre with MADAME RAQUIN's *armchair and the stool.* GRIVET *has just finished a detailed examination of her and is now moving back to his capacious medical bag.*

GRIVET   Thank you, madame. Relax, please. (*He watches her out of the corner of his eye as she lowers her legs to the ground with difficulty.*) The legs don't get much easier, do they?

MME. RAQUIN No, they don't. But why shouldn't they complain? I've been standing on them most of my life.

GRIVET   And the arms?

MME. RAQUIN Stiff. Well, stiffish.

GRIVET   I see. (*Produces pills*) So we'll take one of these thrice daily until the pain eases. Always with food. Plenty of good rich nourishment, that's what we need from now on.

MME. RAQUIN I'll try. But I seldom feel like eating.

Grivet opens up his diary to enter medical details.

GRIVET   Good gracious, we're almost at the end of September.

MME. RAQUIN (*thoughtfully*) Twelve months next Sunday.

GRIVET   Sorry?

MME. RAQUIN Twelve months exactly since I lost my son.

GRIVET   (*checks*) I have a note to send you flowers.

MME. RAQUIN I don't think I'll ever get used to living without him.

GRIVET   Come, come we mustn't give way to these morbid inclinations; that's the worst possible thing for us.

MME. RAQUIN Then what do you suggest *we* do about it?

GRIVET	Get out and about more, for a start.
MME. RAQUIN	(*harshly*) With these apologies for legs?
GRIVET	There are such things as carriages for hire.
MME. RAQUIN	Cabriolets cost a fortune. As for public transport, that's nothing more or less than a struggle for survival. There's no pleasure in it.
GRIVET	Then why not have more people come to you?
MME. RAQUIN	I see all I want of people, down in the shop.
GRIVET	That's not the same. Besides, it's wrong for you still to be working. No good can come out of standing behind that counter and stretching up to those high shelves.
MME. RAQUIN	I can't let Thérèse and Laurent do everything for me.
GRIVET	Then you should get additional help.
MME. RAQUIN	I'm a haberdasher, doctor, not a millionaire.
GRIVET	I'm worried about Thérèse, too. She looks paler every time I see her.
MME. RAQUIN	And unlike me, she won't be helped.

She stands and, using a stick, moves to the sideboard to put the pills away in the top drawer.

GRIVET	(*too casually*) You know, it wouldn't hurt to start your little soirées up again. I have the fondest memories of our old Thursday evenings round that table.
MME. RAQUIN	I've considered it. But when I see us all, sitting there in my mind's eye, it breaks my heart. (*Gently, she takes the box of dominoes out of the drawer.*) The box hasn't been opened since be left us.
GRIVET	(*understandingly*) No.
MME. RAQUIN	Do you remember how proud he was of them? (*Echoes* CAMILLE) 'Ladies and gentlemen — the pieces! And may the best man win' . . . they're real ivory, you know; a present from his father.
GRIVET	I'm sure he'd like them to be used again.

MME. RAQUIN	I don't think I could bear it. No.

She puts back the box and closes the drawer. GRIVET *consciously changes the subject.*

GRIVET	What's happened to Laurent today? He usually brings me up.
MME. RAQUIN	He's out shopping. Dear Laurent . He's here every day God sends.
GRIVET	You're lucky to have found someone so devoted—
MME. RAQUIN	How he finds the time to paint, I'll never know.
GRIVET	He does, nevertheless. (*He shuts up his bag and comes to her.*) I happened to be seeing a patient in the Rue Mazarine the other day, and took the opportunity to call on him. You've visited his studio, I take it?
MME. RAQUIN	Never.
GRIVET	(*surprised*) But he invites everyone.
MME. RAQUIN	He's told me all about it, never fear. An attic, isn't it? With a great big skylight that lets the rain in?
GRIVET	(*carefully*) Has he ever discussed his work with you?
MME. RAQUIN	No, but it doesn't surprise me. He's a solitary artist, very sensitive, and I don't like to ask, I have such a conscience about him and his work.
GRIVET	I shall never forget the sight. The shelves, the floor, even the landing outside, all crammed with canvases. Faces, mostly. Children's faces, women's faces, old men's faces, even the face of an angel. And they all had one thing in common.
MME. RAQUIN	Every painter has an individual style.
GRIVET	This wasn't a style, madame; it was more like an obsession. Every painted face I saw that day reminded me of Camille.
MME. RAQUIN	How could that be?

GRIVET	They all had Camille's eyes, and that little crooked smile of his. Imagine that, an angel with a crooked smile! Whatever he paints, Camille is there on the canvas. It seems you're not the only one with a conscience.
MME. RAQUIN	Oh, the poor boy. Camille stays with him too, then? I'll never forget how I misjudged him on that awful night.
GRIVET	You must have been out of your mind with shock ...
MME. RAQUIN	I was monstrous to him. And how did he repay me? He went to the morgue every single day for almost a fortnight, searching among the bodies. Till one day he recognised my son. I wasn't allowed to go there, they wouldn't let me see him. Michaud did the identification.
GRIVET	I remember. (*Sourly*) And how he revelled in it! Especially that long article in the newspaper.
MME. RAQUIN	I won't hear a word against Michaud; even though he never comes to see me now.
GRIVET	You don't invite him.
MME. RAQUIN	That shouldn't be necessary.
GRIVET	Besides, he's very busily engaged.
MME. RAQUIN	But I thought he'd retired?
GRIVET	He has, of course. But he's started writing a book about his experiences.
MME. RAQUIN	Henri Michaud, an author?
GRIVET	I'm correcting the manuscript for him as he goes along. I'm quite good at grammar and syntax. Why do you smile?
MME. RAQUIN	Nothing to do with you. I was just wondering whether I have the honour of appearing in it. I don't know if I ever told you, but as a young man he was quite attached to me.
GRIVET	He never stops telling everybody. But this is a serious study of crime, not a romantic idyll.

MME. RAQUIN   (*laughs*) Then it won't sell half as many copies!

              LAURENT *comes up the stairs with two bags of
              shopping*

MME. RAQUIN   Hello, Laurent.

LAURENT   What's this — you with a smile on your face?

MME. RAQUIN   The doctor's been making me laugh.

LAURENT   Your jokes must be improving, Grivet. How are
              you?

GRIVET   As well as can be expected of an old man in this
              kind of weather. You're in rude health, I see?

LAURENT   I'm never ill.

              MADAME *half-rises to help him.*

MME. RAQUIN   I'll unpack those in the kitchen.

LAURENT   You'll do no such thing. Stay where you are.

              *She smiles gratefully and settles back again as he takes
              the shopping off.*

MME. RAQUIN   You see? I'm no longer mistress of my own
              house.

GRIVET   He's turning into a second son. Except . . .

MME. RAQUIN   What?

GRIVET   To be frank, madame, I don't remember
              Camille ever showing that degree of
              consideration.

MME. RAQUIN   (*as the smile fades*) I was never as poorly in his
              day.

              LAURENT *returns with a glass of water for her.*

LAURENT   And how do you find madame?

GRIVET   Improved, I'm glad to say. But not as much as
              I'd like. She must rest more.

LAURENT   We'll see she does. (*He hands the water to her with
              a smile.*)

MME. RAQUIN   Thank you, Laurent.

GRIVET	(*picks up bag*) Rest, madame. Not only of body, but of mind too. (*To* LAURENT) Only madame herself can see to that. No sudden shocks and starts, no brooding and no depressions.
MME. RAQUIN	I'll do my best.
GRIVET	I'll look in again soon, though, sadly, not on Thursday evening, eh?
MME. RAQUIN	I'll think about it. I can't promise more than that.
GRIVET	Good-day to you both. (*He leaves them.*)
LAURENT	Thursday?
MME. RAQUIN	He'd like me to start our social evenings up again. What do you think, Laurent? Should I invite them here just once, for old times' sake?
LAURENT	I wouldn't. You'd only work yourself to a shadow and you heard what he just said — no strain, no over-excitement.
MME. RAQUIN	There's no chance of that. You and Thérèse don't let me stir a finger.
LAURENT	We'll find you plenty to do when you're well again.
MME. RAQUIN	And that may give you a chance to paint properly. That's why you came to Paris, after all.
LAURENT	I manage well enough.
MME. RAQUIN	What about that large canvas you were going to have ready for the Exhibition, have you started on it yet?
LAURENT	This year, next year, what's the difference? Your health comes first with me.
MME. RAQUIN	Why do you give so much of your time to me — so much of yourself?
LAURENT	You really want to know?
MME. RAQUIN	(*pressing*) So much of your *freedom* —?
	LAURENT *sits before he answers.*

LAURENT	First, because I can never forgive myself for what I did to you.
MME. RAQUIN	You weren't to blame, Laurent, I've told you a thousand times.
LAURENT	We'd never have gone to St. Ouen that day if I hadn't thought of it.
MME. RAQUIN	So you sacrifice yourself for Camille's memory?
LAURENT	Partly. But it's no sacrifice. I *enjoy* it because, second, you and Thérèse are the only family I have.
	Pause.
MME. RAQUIN	You don't hear from your father any more?
LAURENT	Not a word. He turned his back on me when I deserted the Law for painting. And my father never looks over his shoulder.
MME. RAQUIN	And you have no mother?
LAURENT	She died when I was born. That's why he never liked me.
MME. RAQUIN	Then as your adopted family, we must do our best to be worthy of you.
LAURENT	(*rising*) I'd better get on with some work.
MME. RAQUIN	Wait. First, I have a little surprise for you.
LAURENT	What sort of surprise?
MME. RAQUIN	Starting next week, I'm making you a personal allowance. Fifty francs a month, for as long as I live.
LAURENT	But I don't want paying! Besides, you can't afford it.
MME. RAQUIN	Nonsense. I can manage it quite easily out of the income on my capital. The shop's thriving, and that covers all our living expenses. I know how you have to plan and scheme at the moment.
LAURENT	Scheme, madame?

MME. RAQUIN	To keep that cupboard of a studio going! This will make you a little more independent. You might even afford some new brushes now and a few decent canvases. Make sure you buy one big enough for the Salon.

LAURENT has lowered his head.

LAURENT	I don't take easily to charity.
MME. RAQUIN	This isn't charity. Look on it as a reward — one you've more than earned.
LAURENT	In that case, I accept. And thank you.
MME. RAQUIN	(*rises*) And now I've sat in here ever since lunchtime and I'm tired of these four walls. Hand me my stick, I'm going down to give Thérèse a little rest.
LAURENT	(*hands stick*) Half an hour at the most. If you stay there longer, I'll carry you back myself.
MME. RAQUIN	Bully. She needs the rest much more than I do.

She goes off down the stairs. LAURENT watches her off with pretended solicitude, but the moment he has the room to himself, he drops all pretence. He crosses, smiling broadly, to pick up the glass she has left behind. Whistling merrily, he waltzes it off to the kitchen. THERESE comes up the stairs, looking pale and wan. LAURENT returns.

LAURENT	Thérèse, what do you think? I've come into money.
THERESE	What are you talking about?
LAURENT	The old girl — she's just told me. She's settling fifty francs a month on me from now on.
THERESE	Why would she do a thing like that?
LAURENT	Wages! For coming here and helping you both. (*Laughs*) If only she knew the real reason why I come!
THERESE	Not so loud, she'll hear.
LAURENT	Me drawing a salary! I've never had one before in my life —

THERESE	I'm very happy for you. (*He goes to touch her but she moves away.*) Don't.
LAURENT	Let's go out tonight and celebrate. Somewhere new, and alive — far away from this mausoleum.
THERESE	You know we can't.
LAURENT	(*hardening*) No, I don't.
THERESE	If people saw us out together they might suspect. We have to be so careful.
LAURENT	To hell with being careful — just for once!
THERESE	I said no, Laurent. (*She sits, wearily.*)
LAURENT	I've been careful for a year now, and I'm sick to death of it. We could find somewhere with lights and music, somewhere we could dance. That's one way of holding you in my arms.
THERESE	I'm sorry — no.
LAURENT	You never let me come near you nowadays. You've turned into some sort of ice-maiden ever since —
THERESE	Don't say it. We swore we'd never speak of it in this room.
LAURENT	I have to. I need you, Thérèse.
THERESE	It's just as bad for me. But it can't be long now. Day by day she's moving closer to what we want — that money proves it. But the idea must come from her. Otherwise...
LAURENT	I know you're right. Logic tells me so. But I have feelings, too.
THERESE	We can't show them yet — either of us.
LAURENT	I never dreamed —
THERESE	What?
LAURENT	Oh, never mind.

He goes to gaze gloomily into the fire. THERESE *gets up and follows him.*

THERESE	No doubts. No doubts, my darling — ever. I'm still yours. I always will be.
	He turns to face her.
LAURENT	How long, Thérèse?
THERESE	As long as it takes. You promised.
	The shop-bell goes, downstairs, where we hear MADAME RAQUIN *greet someone happily.*
MME. RAQUIN	(*off*) Thérèse — Laurent! We have a distinguished visitor!
	THERESE *moves swiftly away to the stairhead, as* MADAME RAQUIN *ascends with* MICHAUD, *who carries a carpet-bag.*
MICHAUD	Good afternoon.
LAURENT	What brings you here, monsieur?
MICHAUD	Conscience, my young friend; the iron of the soul.
MME. RAQUIN	He's not only writing books now, he's beginning to talk like one. (*As* MICHAUD *glances sharply*) Yes, I know all about your little secret, you needn't bother to deny it.
MICHAUD	Grivet told you. I expressly forbade him to.
MME. RAQUIN	Why?
MICHAUD	Beause you'll only make fun of me, you always do.
LAURENT	You said something about conscience, monsieur?
MICHAUD	I like you, Laurent, because you never laugh at me. Yes, I was sitting at my desk nibbling on my pen and wondering how I ever came to solve the Longchamps murder alone and unaided, when it suddenly struck me — I hadn't been near this house for over a month.
MME. RAQUIN	Nine and a half weeks, to be precise.
MICHAUD	Is it so long? That's what comes of struggling with a masterpiece, you lose all count of time. Anyway, I went straight out and bought

	presents for you all to make amends. Here...(*delves in bag*) ... Thérèse. (*He hands her a posy of flowers.*)
THERESE	(*kisses him*) They're lovely. Thank you. I'll put them in a vase. (*She takes them off to the kitchen.*)
MICHAUD	Laurent? That was a bit more difficult. But then I thought, 'What man doesn't revel in a good smoke?' So, cheroots, Laurent — and I hope they're to your liking. (*He hands over a box.*)
LAURENT	They're my favourites — when I can afford them. Thank you, Michaud.
MICHAUD	And finally, for madame.
MME. RAQUIN	The last on your list, monsieur?
MICHAUD	Something extra-special. I tramped halfway across Paris to track this down. (*Produces it with a flourish*) One jar of coltsfoot jelly.
MME. RAQUIN	How touching — it's exactly what I wanted.
MICHAUD	(*misses her irony*) That'll have you back on your feet in no time. My mother used to swear by it before she died. (*As they laugh*) Oh dear, that's not what I meant to say at all!
MME. RAQUIN	You'll never change, Henri.
	THERESE *returns with the flowers, now in a small vase. They watch her as she crosses and puts them on the mantelshelf beneath the portrait. It is like an offering.*
MME. RAQUIN	(*in a hushed tone*) She's passed them on to Camille.
MICHAUD	(*thoughtfully*) So I see.
LAURENT	Tell us your news, Michaud. Is it true you're writing a book?
MICHAUD	Yes, and it's coming on splendidly. That's another reason I'm here. I want to browse over my early days, with madame. Would you both excuse us for a quarter of an hour?

THERESE	Certainly. I'm needed in the shop anyway. Coming, Laurent?
LAURENT	Yes, it could do with a tidy-up. And I promised to fix those brackets for you . . .
	The two young ones leave.
MME. RAQUIN	Well, sit down, now you're here — if you can spare the time!
	She indicates a chair with a wave of her stick. He catches hold of the end of it.
MICHAUD	You still need this, then?
MME. RAQUIN	(*nods*) Ever since Camille died.
MICHAUD	I'd hoped it would be a temporary measure.
MME. RAQUIN	Old age makes fools of us all. Your turn will come.
MICHAUD	Talking of old age, I ran into Doctor Grivet at the end of the passage. We had quite a chat.
MME. RAQUIN	Did it come to blows?
MICHAUD	(*chuckles*) Not this time. For once, I found myself entirely in agreement with him. He'd like our Thursday evenings back again — and so should I.
MME. RAQUIN	He asked me, and I said they could never be the same without my son.
MICHAUD	Quite, quite. I understand the problem, madame, but perhaps it's not incapable of solution. (*He has wandered to the fire.*)
MME. RAQUIN	So you haven't come about the book after all? I knew it, by the way you couldn't keep still; you never could, when you were telling lies.
MICHAUD	No, the book can take care of itself. I came to talk to you about Thérèse.
MME. RAQUIN	How do you think my niece is looking?
MICHAUD	Like a wraith.
MME. RAQUIN	Grivet said the same. Sometimes I think he should be attending her instead of me.

MICHAUD	That wouldn't help. Thérèse has a sublime sickness of the soul. Grivet's medicines are powerless against that.
MME. RAQUIN	Life lost all meaning for her when her husband died.
MICHAUD	She's told you as much?
MME. RAQUIN	She doesn't have to. She's like my own flesh and blood.
MICHAUD	Does she talk about it at all?
MME. RAQUIN	Never. If I try, she gets angry and shuts herself away from me like a wounded animal. We're two of a kind, I'm afraid.
MICHAUD	And yet at her age one shouldn't be inconsolable. Did she cry much at first, when it happened?
MME. RAQUIN	Thérèse doesn't cry easily, she never did. What came upon her was a kind of silent agony that lasted for months. Then her nerves began to tell on her.
MICHAUD	Nerves?
MME. RAQUIN	One night — and I haven't told this to anyone — I heard a stifled sobbing in here, and of course came in to see what I could do. She didn't even know who I was. I think she was having some sort of awful nightmare, twisting and turning, muttering away to herself.
MICHAUD	About what?
MME. RAQUIN	Nothing I could make out. But she was calling on Camille constantly. She won't come in here at nights now without a light. In the daytime she's so exhausted she can hardly eat enough to keep a mouse alive. I'm afraid for what may become of her.
MICHAUD	I'll be blunt, madame. Forty years of knowing you have given me that right. The girl must marry again.
MME. RAQUIN	Thérèse? You don't know what you're saying.

MICHAUD	Indeed I do.
MME. RAQUIN	Oh no, Michaud. It would be a kind of sacrilege. You see how she is, she lives in the past. Even your flowers — she offered them straight to Camille. That picture and his memory, that's all she's got left.
MICHAUD	When a woman's afraid to go to her room at night it's because she needs a husband, whether she realises it or not. But realise it she will, as time goes by. By then it may be too late for us to act.
MME. RAQUIN	(*alarmed*) If anyone took her away from me, it would be like losing Camille all over again.
MICHAUD	Don't alarm yourself. There's no question of her leaving here.
MME. RAQUIN	You mean bring a stranger into our home? That would be intolerable.
MICHAUD	No strangers either. What we have to do is find someone you both know and love, who would be a good husband for Thérèse, and a second son to you.
MME. RAQUIN	There's no-one.
MICHAUD	On the contrary, I think you see such a gentleman every day.
	Pause.
MME. RAQUIN	Laurent?
MICHAUD	An admirable choice — why didn't I think of it?
MME. RAQUIN	Thérèse — and Laurent?
MICHAUD	Someone who, I am sure, has already given his heart to her.
MME. RAQUIN	They're fond of each other, I know, but not in that way; they're more like brother and sister.
MICHAUD	Then we must open their eyes for them. I want the three of you to be a family, happy and united. In fact, I want the old days back again and I think this is the way to have them.

MME. RAQUIN We must think of their good, not ours.

MICHAUD That was my primary concern, believe me.

MME. RAQUIN But would we be doing right?

MICHAUD That's for Thérèse to say. Why not broach it to her? I'm sure the young man's mind is half made up for him. The way he looks at her, the way he hangs on her every word ...

MME. RAQUIN I wish I could be sure. I'm old. I can hardly move myself about now. All I ask is to spend my remaining days here in peace and security.

MICHAUD You're forgetting happiness. This could mean happiness, for all three of you. Three dear souls who at the moment are torn apart by an unfortunate and tragic memory.

Pause.

MME. RAQUIN Would such a thing be fair to Camille?

MICHAUD I think he would wish it. Laurent was his greatest friend, and he saved Thérèse's life, don't forget.

MADAME RAQUIN *decides.*

MME. RAQUIN Will you go down and tell Thérèse I want to see her?

MICHAUD With the greatest pleasure. And while she's up here, I'll keep him company in the shop.

He goes downstairs. MADAME RAQUIN *crosses slowly to the portrait.*

MME. RAQUIN Camille, my son ... will you ever forgive me?

She looks up at him beseechingly — it is almost a prayer — and then hobbles back to her chair and sits with her hands clasped over her stick. THERESE *comes quietly up the stairs, her head bent.*

THERESE Michaud said you wanted to see me.

MME. RAQUIN Yes, my child. You've hardly spoken a word all day. What's wrong, Thérèse?

THERESE Nothing. No more than usual.

MME. RAQUIN	Both my old friends have remarked on how ill you look.
THERESE	I'm tired, that's all. Just very, very tired. (*She walks slowly over to the portrait.*)
MME. RAQUIN	Is it your heart, perhaps? Or your chest?
THERESE	No. I don't know. It's just that everything inside me seems empty . . . finished . . . numb.
MME. RAQUIN	Dear Thérèse. (*She pulls herself to her feet and crosses to her niece.*)
THERESE	There's nothing you or anyone can do. It's never going to go away. (*She sighs and sits in* CAMILLE's *armchair.*)
MME. RAQUIN	I can't bear to see you like this, my child. You're all I have now.
THERESE	It's no easier for you. Can you forget Camille, and how he left us?
MME. RAQUIN	Never. (*Gently*) But we're not here to talk about my grief. It's you who must be consoled.
THERESE	Tell me honestly — can anything console *you*? (*A pause, then* MADAME RAQUIN *shakes her head.*) You see? Please let me go now, it hurts to talk about it. (*She rises.*)
MME. RAQUIN	You live too much within yourself.
THERESE	I'm not complaining. Have you ever heard me complain? I had my fair share of happiness before it was snatched away from me.
MME. RAQUIN	I'm old. I have the time to grieve. You're young, you're not yet thirty. You must find yourself again, through others.
THERESE	What others? There's no-one but you in my life.
MME. RAQUIN	You have a future to consider. Do you want to spend the rest of your days widowed and childless?
THERESE	Such things are decided for us by God. They have to be. We have no say.

MME. RAQUIN	Listen to me — and don't fly into a rage. I've been talking things over with Michaud.
THERESE	(*bridles*) What things?
MME. RAQUIN	We care about you, deeply, both of us. He thinks as I do, that you should marry again.

THERESE *stares at her and then violently shakes her head.*

THERESE	Never.
MME. RAQUIN	I told him you'd say that, but he persisted. And he's right, Thérèse: there should be room for more than blackness in any young person's heart.
THERESE	Michaud has no business meddling in my private affairs.
MME. RAQUIN	I asked you not to be angry.
THERESE	What else do you expect? Talking me over like a piece of merchandise in my own home — and with outsiders.
MME. RAQUIN	I knew him before you were born. Won't you even consider it?
THERESE	I don't need to. Someone of my blood can only fall in love once. Then it's for ever.
MME. RAQUIN	There are different kinds of love, Thérèse. We learn that as we grow older.
THERESE	There's point in discussing this.
MME. RAQUIN	Very well. The subject is closed.

She moves away and sits again. THERESE, *not wanting the matter to end there, hovers uncertainly.*

THERESE	I suppose you've got someone all ready and waiting? Who is he — what's he like?
MME. RAQUIN	You know me better than I thought.
THERESE	I know Michaud. He's nothing if not thorough.
MME. RAQUIN	You may as well hear it all. We'd like you to marry Laurent.
THERESE	(*secretly delighted*) Laurent!

MME. RAQUIN	Can't you see how suitable he is? And he loves you, we're sure of that.
THERESE	But I don't love him and I don't want to love him. He wouldn't want it either.
MME. RAQUIN	Suppose he were to ask you, what would you say?
THERESE	What I've said to you. Look at me, I'm still in mourning. All I ask is to go on mourning the man who loved me to the grave. It's wicked of you to try and change my life.
MME. RAQUIN	Is it so wicked to want to see young people smile again? To find a kind of happiness together? Is that too much to ask?
THERESE	I've always tried to please you in everything I've done. I've never gone against your wishes. But this!
MME. RAQUIN	You could at least think about it.
THERESE	Even that seems like a betrayal.
MME. RAQUIN	Camille wouldn't see it as such. He'd want it too.
THERESE	But why?
MME. RAQUIN	Because he can no longer bring you happiness — only grief and sorrow. He'd see it as a new beginning, for all of us. Have you the courage, Thérèse? You've never lacked courage before.
THERESE	A new beginning . . .
MME. RAQUIN	Only you can make it possible.
THERESE	(*going closer*) I've never denied you anything, all the years I've known you.
MME. RAQUIN	And this means more than anything I have ever asked.
	Pause.
THERESE	(*quietly*) Why couldn't you leave me alone with my heartbreak?
MME. RAQUIN	Because I am sixty years of age. You're only thirty. So you'll agree? For all our sakes?

THERESE	*(hesitantly)* If Laurent wants it so — I won't stand in the way.
MME. RAQUIN	Oh, my dear. *(She puts her arms around her niece.)*
LAURENT	*(off)* Madame — Madame Raquin!
	He runs up the stairs with a handsome bouquet of flowers.
LAURENT	Another present for you — not coltsfoot jelly this time!
MME. RAQUIN	What have I done to deserve these?
LAURENT	*(laughs)* They're not from me. Michaud sent them — he said something about congratulations.
	She smiles to herself.
MME. RAQUIN	See to them, Thérèse.
	THERESE *takes the flowers and, as if she cannot meet* LAURENT'S *gaze, hurries off into the kitchen.*
LAURENT	He made me go with him to the shop next door.
MME. RAQUIN	I thought he wanted to talk to you about something important?
LAURENT	He did. And being Michaud, he came straight out with it.
MME. RAQUIN	Did you give him an answer?
LAURENT	There's only one — but I don't think Thérèse would ever listen to me.
MME. RAQUIN	I've just put it to her — and she's accepted.
LAURENT	*(eyes widening)* It can't be true. *(Shouts)* Thérèse, come back here!
	THERESE *re-enters.*
THERESE	What's all this noise?
LAURENT	Is it true? *Will* you marry me? (THERESE *goes and stands at the portrait, looking up at it.*) She never meant it, madame. She's as far away from me as ever.

THERESE	(*turns*) I never say anything I don't mean, Laurent. We have a duty to make our mother happy. I'll be your wife.

LAURENT *takes a quick pace towards her and then hesitates.*

MME. RAQUIN	Kiss her, you idiot! Kiss her before she melts away out of sheer embarrassment.

LAURENT *plants a chaste kiss on* THERESE'S *forehead.*

MME. RAQUIN	On the lips, man — call yourself a Frenchman?

The lovers now embrace properly, to her delight.

LAURENT	Thank you, madame. A thousand times.
MME. RAQUIN	You're sure, Thérèse?
THERESE	It's for the best. I know that now.
MME. RAQUIN	Be a good and faithful wife. Laurent, only you can make her smile again. Camille will thank you for it.

THERESE'S *hand feels for that of* LAURENT, *in silent triumph.*

CURTAIN

Scene Two

Midnight, six weeks later. The room is in darkness, except for the firelight's glow. The clock outside is striking twelve, as MICHAUD *and* GRIVET *climb up the stairs like two conspirators. Both have imbibed freely, but* GRIVET *is the more affected by this.* MICHAUD *lights the main lamp.*

MICHAUD	Let there be light . . . and there was light.
GRIVET	My umbrella. I must put my umbrella somewhere safe.

He attempts to prop it up in its usual corner. It falls down. In retrieving it, GRIVET *almost falls down himself, ending up on his knees.*

MICHAUD	Stand up, my friend; we've done enough praying for one day. Let me help.

He assists him to a chair, where GRIVET *collapses, takes out a large silk handkerchief and sniffs into it.*

GRIVET   Thank you. I'm sorry, weddings always have the strangest effect on me.

He blows his nose noisily as MICHAUD *studies him, poker-faced.*

MICHAUD   Outside in the cab you were singing your heart out. Now you're bawling your head off. Why?

GRIVET   Thérèse and Laurent . . . such a handsome couple. They looked so innocent — so unspotted.

MICHAUD   And that reminded you of your misspent youth. I understand. (*He crosses to make the fire up.*)

GRIVET   No, you don't. I don't mourn for myself; I mourn for what Life may do to them.

MICHAUD   They'll never end up like you, so they'll avoid the worst. Now give me the nettles.

GRIVET   The what?

MICHAUD   The nettles, man! Before the others get here.

GRIVET   I forgot.

He half-rises, to grope inside one of his tail-pockets. Finally he brings out a bunch of crumpled nettles.

MICHAUD   Have they been there all the time — in your tail-pocket?

GRIVET   (*nods blearily*) Ever since we picked them outside the restaurant.

MICHAUD   You sat on them throughout that dreary meal?

GRIVET   Throughout. To keep our guilty secret.

MICHAUD   How are you feeling?

GRIVET   I've got a posterior like a pin-cushion. (*He sits again, very gingerly.*)

MICHAUD   I'm told it's good for rheumatism.

GRIVET   I haven't got rheumatism! Not there, anyway.

| MICHAUD | Then look upon it as preventive medicine. I shall now put these little beauties where they belong. |

He crosses to the bedroom alcove, eases a curtain back, and buries the nettles in the beautifully made bed.

GRIVET	Would you believe it? I nearly got married once. Several times.
MICHAUD	To different ladies?
GRIVET	(*sadly*) Always the same one.

He sniffs into the handkerchief again. MICHAUD *has produced his pocket-flask.*

MICHAUD	And why did you never take the fatal step?
GRIVET	Because — for some incalculable reason — she didn't want to marry me. Can you understand that?
MICHAUD	Perhaps it's something to do with your profession. I never knew a woman yet who trusted doctors. Santé.

He sits near his friend and takes a healthy swig from his flask before offering it to the doctor.

GRIVET	I'd better not. I must maintain my dignity in front of the others. Michaud, do you think they stand at least a fighting chance of happiness?
MICHAUD	Why not? They're admirably suited.
GRIVET	But the marriage has been, to a certain extent, arranged.
MICHAUD	It's better than no marriage at all. Besides, I sometimes think there's no such thing as happiness. When we think we're happy, it's only that we're a little less unhappy than usual.
GRIVET	You're a philosopher.
MICHAUD	I know.
GRIVET	And you're a cynic.
MICHAUD	I know that too.
GRIVET	But I still like you.

MICHAUD	I never knew that before.
	The shop-bell sounds.
GRIVET	Someone's coming! What about the nettles? (*He half-rises again.*)
MICHAUD	Sit down, you fool; it's all been taken care of.
	They sit like two angels as THERESE *and* MADAME RAQUIN *ascend the stairs.*
MME. RAQUIN	So here you are?
MICHAUD	Welcome home, ladies.
	THERESE *is calm and quiet and has only a demure smile for them both.*
GRIVET	My dear, dear friends.
	He rises, sweeps off his hat and sits again, all in one movement, and then finds he is sitting on his hat.
MICHAUD	You must forgive him. I've never seen him quite so carried away.
MME. RAQUIN	I should hope not.
MICHAUD	(*indicates*) The lamps are lit, madame, the fire blazes, and the marital couch awaits. (GRIVET *emits a high-pitched giggle.*) Have I said something funny?
GRIVET	Of course! I mean, of course not.
MME. RAQUIN	Thank you for your help.
MICHAUD	Now that my duties are complete, all that remains is for me to wish all future happiness to all concerned — and to kiss the bride.
MME. RAQUIN	For the fifth time since dinner?
MICHAUD	One never tires of paradise. (*He kisses* THERESE *fondly.*)
THERESE	Thank you, monsieur.
MME. RAQUIN	Now you must leave us in peace. We have a lot to do before the bridegroom gets back.
MICHAUD	I was wondering — a dish of tea, perhaps?

MME. RAQUIN	It wouldn't sit easily on the wine, and Doctor Grivet needs his bed. Don't you realise, you're keeping Thérèse waiting?
MICHAUD	Laurent isn't even here yet!
MME. RAQUIN	Have you forgotten *everything* about Vernon? He mustn't see the bride till she's undressed.
MICHAUD	What a charming thought. Can I be of any assistance?
MME. RAQUIN	No, you cannot. Now off with you both.
MICHAUD	Grivet! Get your umbrella.
	GRIVET *wakes from a doze and totters over for it.*
MME. RAQUIN	Wait. (*She has noticed the open curtain at the alcove and now looks back at* MICHAUD.) You wouldn't dare.
MICHAUD	Dare what, madame?
MME. RAQUIN	Perhaps you *do* remember Vernon, after all.
	She marches over to the bed and finds the nettles.
MICHAUD	Now how on earth did those get there?
MME. RAQUIN	They weren't there when I made the bed, monsieur. Look, Thérèse, see what they were going to do to you? Villains.
GRIVET	Good gracious, that looks exactly like a bunch of nettles.
MME. RAQUIN	Because that's exactly what it is — and that's exactly where it belongs. (*She dumps them in a waste-basket.*)
MICHAUD	Well, it was a damned good idea while it lasted.
MME. RAQUIN	(*laughing*) Now will you please take yourselves off home?
GRIVET	Goodnight, Thérèse. (*Kisses her hand*) I hope your marriage will be a great success.
MME. RAQUIN	Why shouldn't it be?
GRIVET	One feels a certain responsibility.
MICHAUD	Come on, Grivet. Goodnight, ladies.

GRIVET *puts on his battered hat and follows.*

GRIVET   After all, if I hadn't brought the two of them together.

MICHAUD   (*stops in his tracks*) You did *what*?

MME. RAQUIN Good*night*, gentlemen.

GRIVET   (*starts downstairs*) Who thought of it in the first place?

MICHAUD   *I* thought of it. If I hadn't come round here to see madame . . .

GRIVET   Only at my instigation . . .

             Their voices die away as they leave, still arguing.

MME. RAQUIN And now, my dear . . .

THERESE ·   Now I know why they call it a marriage market.

MME. RAQUIN You'd better . . .

THERESE   Let me be; just for a moment. (*She sits in the green armchair.*)

MME. RAQUIN As you wish.

THERESE   What with two ceremonies, then that long drive, then the meal in the restaurant with all the wine and speeches . . .

MME. RAQUIN You must be quite worn out.

THERESE   What about you? You haven't stopped all day.

MME. RAQUIN God provides extra strength when you work for others.

             She returns to the alcove and turns down the bed, afterwards fluffing up the pillows. THERESE *sits still and silent, almost morose. Then she looks slowly round the room.*

THERESE   I could have wished —

MME. RAQUIN What?

THERESE   Nothing.

             MADAME RAQUIN *brings her robe.*

MME. RAQUIN Laurent said he'd be half an hour at the most.

THERESE	I'm not ready yet. Let's talk.
	Her aunt sets the robe to warm by the fire and then transfers a bowl of roses from the living room to the bedside table.
MME. RAQUIN	Everything went off very well, didn't you think? And what a pleasure to see the Mayor in his full regalia!
THERESE	(*with the ghost of a smile*) When he began to read from his little red book, I daren't look at Laurent. He looked so pompous.
MME. RAQUIN	Laurent kept his head bent most of the time.
THERESE	I noticed. He's very shy, in public.
	MADAME RAQUIN *brings brush and comb and* THERESE'S *slippers from the alcove.*
MME. RAQUIN	Anyway, I much preferred the church service. I couldn't help it, the tears were rolling down my cheeks.
THERESE	Women take these things much more seriously than men.
MME. RAQUIN	And your man's going to be here before very long.
THERESE	All right.
	She stands obediently, and allows her aunt to help her off with her dress.
MME. RAQUIN	I cried so much at my own wedding, I could hardly make the responses. That one took even longer.
THERESE	It couldn't have.
MME. RAQUIN	Jean-Pierre stood up so straight and strong, and looked the priest full in the face. (*Pricks herself*) Oh dear, that was a pin. (*Searches for it*) I should remember where it is, I put it in myself. Shall I go and get Michaud to help?
THERESE	He's probably still arguing with Grivet, out in the street.

MME. RAQUIN	Those two! But they're quite inseparable, really. Ah, I've got it.
	She releases the pin and the dress is easily slipped off.
THERESE	Thank you.
	She proceeds to take off her corselet and petticoat. MADAME RAQUIN *is admiring the wedding-dress.*
MME. RAQUIN	It's so lovely, this grey silk. And so beautifully finished! It could stand up by itself. How nervous you are, Thérèse — you're positively shaking.
THERESE	I think I have a cold coming on.
MME. RAQUIN	Not on your wedding night; it's just good, old-fashioned modesty.
	She puts the dress and other things away in the wardrobe cupboard.
THERESE	At least Michaud left us a good fire. (*She warms herself at it.*)
MME. RAQUIN	Now we'll do your hair.
THERESE	I can do it.
MME. RAQUIN	It's my privilege. (*As* THERESE *sits again*) Put your head down, that's right. You're so lucky, you've been blessed with lovely hair. (*Brushes it tenderly*) It suits you to have it down, you look like a princess in a fairy-story. Now I'll roll it up in the neck.
THERESE	Leave it loose. If you'd just tie it back.
	MADAME RAQUIN *does so, with a white ribbon.*
MME. RAQUIN	Beautiful.
THERESE	I could have wished it wasn't winter. And not in this room. In Vernon, in May, the acacias are in full bloom and the nights are warm.
MME. RAQUIN	It was May the last time you — (*halts abruptly*) There, you see how elegant you look? (*Offers mirror*) Now put on your nice, new dressing-gown.

She puts away the brush, comb and mirror, as
THERESE *does as she is bid.*

THERESE You've been so extravagant with us. (*She snuggles
into the robe.*)

MME. RAQUIN Oh, you're like a real bride now — all that lace!
Now I'm going to leave you to prepare yourself.

THERESE (*urgently*) Wait till he comes, please; I think
there's something else we have to say to each
other. (*She glances at the portrait of* CAMILLE.)

MME. RAQUIN (*sternly*) No, nothing. I haven't allowed myself
one word all day, you must have noticed it.

THERESE Yes, and I was thankful while the others were
there. Still —

MME. RAQUIN The past is something to be locked away.
Anything else would be unfair to Laurent.

THERESE Yes — mother.

The shop-bell sounds.

THERESE He's here.

MME. RAQUIN That bell should have been taken off the hook.
In all the excitement we forgot.

LAURENT *comes up the stairs, singing softly to himself.
He carries a bottle of vintage champagne.*

LAURENT Here I am, then, and this is the last bottle we
had left —

He stops as he catches sight of THERESE.

MME. RAQUIN There, Laurent. What do you think of your
bride now?

LAURENT (*breathes*) I think she's the loveliest creature God
ever made.

THERESE *turns away to the fire.*

MME. RAQUIN The future's bright now. I know you won't
leave me to go off on honeymoon, but as soon as
I'm strong enough, we're all going away, for an
extra-special holiday.

LAURENT Where to?

THERESE	(*as if she knows*) Vernon.
MME. RAQUIN	Yes — how did you guess? You'll love Normandy, Laurent. In spring-time the mimosa lights up the valleys like a million lanterns.
LAURENT	That's something I must paint.
MME. RAQUIN	You will. You'll paint everything. Goodnight — my son.
LAURENT	Goodnight. And thank you for everything. For all the new clothes, for that wonderful reception and most of all — for her.
	THERESE *crosses in silence to kiss her aunt.*
THERESE	You've been too good to us. I mean that.
MME. RAQUIN	Be happy, my children. Goodnight.
	She leaves them. Pause.
LAURENT	Thérèse, my darling.
THERESE	Wait, Laurent.
LAURENT	What's the matter?
THERESE	I'm not ready. And it's so cold in here. (*She moves away from him.*)
LAURENT	Go back to the fire.
	She returns to the green armchair and he stands admiring her before moving away to take off his jacket and waistcoat. Then he goes to kneel by her.
LAURENT	Married. Legally married. Can you realise it? I can't — not yet. (*He takes her hand to look at her wedding ring.*) And there's the proof. You're trembling!
THERESE	It's been a year now — over. It's only natural that I should be nervous.
LAURENT	Nervous of me?
THERESE	I can't explain it, even to myself. But it's as if — as if we'd never met before. Not our real selves. As if we came together, two strangers in darkness, and only now . . .
LAURENT	I know a first-class cure for that.

He rises from her and goes over to open the champagne.

THERESE   I'm not the only one. It was on your mind too, all through the ceremony. Especially in church.

LAURENT   There's nothing wrong with me that a drink won't put right.

THERESE   So you drink not because you want to but because you need to?

LAURENT   I drink because I like it.

THERESE   Don't pretend. It hasn't come to that, has it?

LAURENT   What's wrong with you, Thérèse?

THERESE   We're both talking for the sake of talking, don't you feel that? We haven't had the courage to kiss each other yet. But you're afraid you'll look a fool if you don't kiss me, aren't you? If we don't make love. That's so stupid. We're not ordinary married people, we don't have to pretend to each other.

LAURENT   I'm ordinary. I don't know about you, but I'm an ordinary man, having an ordinary drink on the most extraordinary evening of his life. And I'd like my wife to join me. (*He holds out her glass.*)

THERESE   In a moment.

She crosses to the arch, where she stands listening anxiously.

LAURENT   Who's being stupid now?

THERESE   I just want to be sure she's sleeping.

LAURENT   Thérèse, we don't have to worry about other people any more . . .

THERESE   (*not immediately*) I'm sorry. If you want the truth, I suddenly realised that almost ever since I came in, I've been sitting over there — in Camille's chair.

Pause.

LAURENT   I see. That kind of nervousness.

He pushes the chair with his foot so that it rolls clear of them.

THERESE   Be patient with me; I'll be myself in a minute or two. It was only the chair.

LAURENT   Oh, damn the chair! Have your drink.

THERESE *sips her champagne and then puts the glass down.*

THERESE   (*making conversation*) Do you think we really shall go to Vernon?

LAURENT   How should I know? And why should I care? (*He drinks deeply.*)

THERESE   Don't sulk. I'd love to show it to you.

LAURENT   Vernon in the Spring — how many times have I heard that little love-song? I suppose it was in the Spring when you married before?

THERESE *looks as though he has hit her.*

THERESE   It was springtime when I first went there and found a home.

LAURENT   And there the conversation ended. (*He goes to refill his glass.*)

THERESE   What time is it?

LAURENT   Getting on for one.

THERESE   What a long day it's been. Are you the same as I am, Laurent? I don't like being in cabs very much. I'd sooner go on foot.

LAURENT   I like anything that's expensive.

THERESE   Driving about for hours bores me to tears. What's more, I hate eating out in restaurants.

LAURENT   I agree with you there — unless it's by the water. There's something about those little riverside inns — (*stops*)

THERESE   Underneath all you say, I hear other words. While you're talking I can hear your thoughts. You'd got as far as the accident, hadn't you?

LAURENT   (*sharply*) I thought we weren't supposed to talk
            about that?

            *She now sits on the stool and presses her hands to her
            head.*

THERESE   Do as I'm doing. Shut your eyes. Force yourself
            to think of nothing.

            Pause.

LAURENT   Thérèse, for God's sake say something —
            anything!

THERESE   Even when I'm doing this, I think. I can't *not*
            think. (*Opens her eyes*) Silence doesn't work. One
            must talk. (*She gets up, forcing a brightness she is far
            from feeling.* LAURENT *does his best to fall in with her
            subterfuge.*) The Town Hall was freezing this
            afternoon.

LAURENT   Freezing.

THERESE   The only warm place all day was that little
            grating in the floor of the church. Did you see it
            — quite close to where we knelt?

LAURENT   Grivet planted himself on top of it as soon as we
            moved to the altar. He looked triumphant, the
            old devil.

THERESE   At first. Only at first. Then he kept crying.

LAURENT   I know. I couldn't look at him.

THERESE   I daren't look at you.

            They both try to laugh but it is a miserable failure.

LAURENT   The church was too dark. That was the weather.
            Weddings ought to be in sunshine.

THERESE   Sunshine, yes.

LAURENT   Did you see the lace on the altar-cloth?

THERESE   Worth ten francs a metre at least. There's
            nothing so good in the shop.

LAURENT   And the smell of incense. It always turns my
            stomach.

THERESE   He was just the same, he — (*stops herself, gasping*)

LAURENT	(*quickly*) At first I thought we were the only people there, in that great empty building. Just our little wedding party. Everything echoing all around us. Then the echoes became a chant. People chanting. You must have seen them, in that chapel across the nave?
THERESE	(*nods*) People with tapers.
LAURENT	A funeral!
THERESE	When I raised my eyes, I saw the black pall, with a great white cross. The coffin passed quite close to us. (*Whispers*) I saw it. A little, narrow, shabby coffin. Some poor creature. (*They have drawn quite close now. Suddenly her head goes on his shoulder.*) When you went to the morgue ... you saw him? Really saw him?
LAURENT	I saw him.
THERESE	You saw his face? It wasn't just the clothes?
LAURENT	On the tenth day I went there, I saw his face.
THERESE	Did he look as if he'd suffered?
LAURENT	(*deep in memory*) Horribly.
THERESE	His eyes were open, weren't they?
LAURENT	Staring at me.
THERESE	I've tried to imagine —
LAURENT	Like a visitation from hell. The face was mottled blue, and swollen. Grinning. The corner of his mouth all twisted up.
	He feels at his throat, where CAMILLE *bit him on the night of the murder.*
THERESE	Tell me everything. I must suffer what you've suffered. On the nights when I can't sleep I can never see him clearly, and I must. *I must see him.*
LAURENT	Damn his memory!
	He pulls violently away from her and tears off his collar and cravat.
THERESE	Laurent —

LAURENT   It hurts where he bit me — hurts. (*Looks at his finger wonderingly*) It's bleeding . . .

THERESE   The collar's chafed it, that's all.

LAURENT   It means —

THERESE   Nothing! Let me make it better. (*Kisses the spot, then recoils*) It burns me!

            He takes hold of her.

LAURENT   Put this out of your mind. I saw nothing in the morgue. Keep telling yourself that. We'll make ourselves believe it —

THERESE   I knew the thoughts would break through, they had to. Everything we talked about led up to it: Vernon in the Spring, the riverside inns, that miserable little coffin. We can never talk of ordinary things again, Camille's made sure of that.

LAURENT   He's dead. Camille can't hurt us now.

THERESE   He's here with us — here in this room. He's all around us. He had you by the throat!

LAURENT   Don't go on like this, it's madness —

            She breaks away from him and goes back to the fire.

THERESE   Send him away, Laurent. For God's sake, send him away!

LAURENT   I know how, We'll turn the clock back. We won't be man and wife, we'll be Thérèse and Laurent, all over again. (*He goes for his coat.*)

THERESE   Don't leave me!

LAURENT   Only for a moment. Downstairs, through the shop, along the passage as far as our door. When you hear the signal, let me in.

THERESE   Yes — oh yes, my darling — please!

LAURENT   Be ready. (*He urges her gently towards the alcove.*)

THERESE   Don't forget the bell. If she hears that she might come in.

LAURENT   I'll quieten it. (*Keeping up the charade*) We don't
               want anyone to find out now.

               *He closes the curtains on her. Then he looks round the
               room, breathing hard. He crosses to pour another drink
               and tosses it back in a single gulp. He goes off down
               the stairs, and the room is still and quiet as the clock
               outside strikes one.* THERESE *parts the curtains, unlocks
               the alcove door and comes back into the room, barefooted
               now and wearing only her nightdress. She puts out the
               lamp so that the only illumination now comes from the
               moonlight and the glowing embers. As she stares up at
               the portrait of her first husband, it seems to shine with
               an unearthly light.* LAURENT's *shape appears outside
               the windows and he knocks three times, softly, on the
               glass door.* THERESE *moves to the door and opens it but
               shrinks back as he steps into the room.* LAURENT *holds
               out his arms to her. She is shaking her head slowly.*

THERESE   Green. Everything's green tonight. Camille's
               chair. The wine bottle. Now the moonlight on
               your face. Close the curtains, shut it out!

               *He swishes the curtains together and the room is now
               bathed only in the soft glow from the fire. He comes to*
               THERESE *and takes her in his arms. Her body is rigid
               and unyielding.*

LAURENT   Thérèse ... you're my wife.

THERESE   (*whispers*) Useless. I can't feel your touch. (*Backs
               out of his grasp*) We're not in love any more.

LAURENT   I've waited, and I've suffered, more than a
               year. I've built my whole life round tonight.

THERESE   We killed love.

LAURENT   (*desperately*) That's only your fancy. It's late and
               you're tired. Now put your arms around me,
               hold me close.

THERESE   No, no, it's asking for sorrow. If we made love
               now, Camille would be here with us, laughing at
               us, cursing us!

LAURENT   (*advancing*) He shan't have you back.

THERESE	(*turns, cowering*) Don't. Don't come near me.
LAURENT	It's that damned picture. You've lived with it too much. I want it down, I want it out of here.

He sweeps her aside and THERESE *falls with a cry against* CAMILLE'S *armchair as* LAURENT *tears the picture down in a fury. Neither of them notices that* MADAME RAQUIN *has come quietly out of her bedroom and is standing at the corner of the archway, listening.*

LAURENT	I created this, and I can destroy it. (*Holding the thing in front of him, he lets all the hatred pour out of him.*) Curse you, Camille. I threw you in the river and held you down till you were dead. Now you come back from hell to haunt us both —

A hoarse scream comes from MADAME RAQUIN.

MME. RAQUIN	Murderers!

The lovers turn to stare at her as she goes towards them menacingly.

MME. RAQUIN	You killed my son. My son! (*Suddenly her face contorts in agony and she puts a hand to her heart.*) God damn you both!

Another seizure strikes her, taking her speech. Her arms hang limply as she sits, powerless, her chest heaving.

LAURENT	She can't move.
THERESE	We were warned — her mouth!
LAURENT	All twisted up, like Camille's.

MADAME RAQUIN'S *breath rasps harshly in her throat.*

THERESE	Is she dying?
LAURENT	No. Look at those eyes — they're alive with hate.
THERESE	May God turn her lips and hands to stone.

CURTAIN

ACT THREE

Evening, some months later.

There is now an air of general dilapidation over the whole room. CAMILLE'S portrait has vanished from over the fireplace and the old landscape is back once more. The bed in the alcove has been replaced by a narrow truckle affair, which has been left carelessly unmade, the bedclothes in an untidy heap. The table has been moved back to Centre and some windows are open, though the weather is wintry.

LAURENT pushes a wheelchair in through the arch. In it is MADAME RAQUIN. She is dressed from head to foot in black and is now completely paralysed.

LAURENT This is what you need, a little change of scene. (*Settles her near table*) All right there? Now we'll close the windows and get rid of some of the draught. I know how you hate cold air, and it's not the time of year for open windows. (*He closes windows and lights the lamp.*) I spoil you, don't I? You don't get this sort of attention from her, you know. You could rot in that old bedroom of yours for all she cares. Self, self, self, — that's all it is with her.

    THERESE struggles up from below with a couple of extra chairs.

LAURENT Hello — are your ears burning? We were just talking about you.

THERESE I asked you three times to bring these up for me.

LAURENT I was feeding her.

THERESE Why am I always left to do the donkey-work?

LAURENT It's your own fault. You should never have started these Thursday evenings up again.

THERESE We had to — *we*. Everything must appear as normal as possible. Anything else is dangerous.

LAURENT If you ask me, it's a damned sight more dangerous to let those two back into our lives.

THERESE	One's her doctor and the other's her oldest friend. What do you want me to do, bar them from the house? That *would* give people something to talk about.
LAURENT	All right! Grivet's got to come, I know. But why Michaud?
THERESE	As normal as possible, I said.
LAURENT	I don't trust him and never have. Once a policeman, always a policeman.
THERESE	Oh, I see. Michaud's no threat. He lives in a world of his own nowadays.
LAURENT	So you say. He always seems sharp enough when he comes here. The way he picks up the least little thing.
THERESE	(*dismissing it*) I thought you were supposed to be cleaning up in here?
LAURENT	I've only got one pair of hands.
THERESE	Look at that bed of yours — why the hell don't you make it in the mornings?

LAURENT *crosses and slings the covers roughly into place, afterwards drawing the curtains on it.*

LAURENT	Separate beds, separate lives. What's normal about that?
THERESE	I have to be with her during the nights.
LAURENT	It doesn't matter any more. I'm getting used to our kind of normality by now.
THERESE	(*crosses to sideboard*) They'll be here soon and you haven't even got the wine yet.
LAURENT	I've been waiting for some wine money.
THERESE	I'm getting it. (*She unlocks the top drawer and takes out a cash-box.*)
LAURENT	We ought to offer them a bite to eat as well. There always used to be cakes in the old days.
THERESE	The housekeeping won't run to it. Here. Two francs will have to do.

LAURENT	(*takes coins*) What sort of vinegar can I buy for two francs?
THERESE	Malaga. We can't afford the Chablis any more. *She locks the box away.*
LAURENT	Michaud's going to love that.
THERESE	Times have changed. He'll just have to put up with it.
LAURENT	If you were a bit more organised — sent some accounts out now and then, and stocked a few new lines ... Madame knew how to run a shop; we were always in profit in her day.
THERESE	Perhaps you'd like to find the time to do it for me?
LAURENT	Perhaps I'd like to find the time to do some painting. (*He lounges towards the stairs.*)
THERESE	And take the bell off the hook while you're down there.
LAURENT	I may be only the hired help now, but I don't take orders, Thérèse. From you or anyone.
THERESE	Please.
LAURENT	That's better.

He leaves. THERESE *sets to work to tidy the room, talking sporadically to the hunched figure in the wheelchair.*

THERESE	Dirt, that's all I am, these days, He treats me like dirt. I used to have a bit of self-respect. That's gone now, like everything else. I should have known the kind of man he was from the beginning. He only came here in the first place to get a free bed and as much food and drink as he could stuff down himself. Laurent the Pig! And he hasn't changed underneath. It's a good thing they gave me the power to act for you, and not Laurent the Pig. He'd like to get his hands on our money but he'll never do that. I only keep enough in the house to live on; the rest is in the bank, where it belongs. He'd run

through it in no time, what with his drinking and his 'little outings', as he's pleased to call them. (*She sets the chairs in place at the table.*) And making me lift heavy furniture about, just like a servant! It was never like this with Camille. Whatever his faults, he always treated me like a lady. Look at me now! (*She checks her appearance in the mirror.*) I'm old. I'm haggard. He'd never have let this happen to me. But then he was a gentleman, born and bred. But this one! And going on like that about the shop. I know you were better behind the counter — you've been in business all your life — but Camille always did the paperwork for you and there was never a penny out of place. That's why we prospered. It wasn't an ideal marriage but it was peaceful enough until he brought this monster into our lives. (*She goes to the old lady and now talks directly at her.*) I wish I knew how much of all this you can take in. Sitting there watching us all day long. Can you ever understand a single word we say?

LAURENT's *voice breaks in on her reverie.*

LAURENT	(*calls, off*) We're here, Thérèse!

He comes up the stairs with MICHAUD, *who carries bottles of wine in a paper bag.*

THERESE	(*flustered*) You're early, monsieur.
LAURENT	He caught me going into the wine shop and wouldn't let me buy anything. Everything's been provided for, he says.
MICHAUD	(*jovially*) And so it has. I brought it with me.

He unloads his bottles on to the table.

THERESE	I don't understand.
MICHAUD	One ... two ... three. Chablis, the best there is.
THERESE	You bought the wine last time.
MICHAUD	And I've bought it this time.
THERESE	How much do we owe you?

MICHAUD	Not a sou. I've just had a handsome advance from my publisher, and money was made for spending.
THERESE	(*takes his hat*) You're very good to us. I promise you, when the shop's doing better —
MICHAUD	(*brushes this aside*) How's madame tonight?
LAURENT	There's no change.
THERESE	It's a cruel, heartless thing, paralysis. Sitting there in that chair all day long, never moving a muscle. It's like being buried alive.
LAURENT	Sometimes we think she might be better off if —
MICHAUD	Don't say that. Look at those eyes, Laurent. They burn with life. Besides, there's always a chance she may return to something like normal.
LAURENT	Grivet maintains there's very little hope.
MICHAUD	It still exists. He said in the beginning that she might regain the use of her limbs one day, if only partially.
LAURENT	I suppose it's been known, but ...
MICHAUD	Why, she might even learn to speak again, given time.
THERESE	(*startled*) Grivet said that?
MICHAUD	Of course, it's only an outside chance.
LAURENT	He's never mentioned a word of this to us.
MICHAUD	Probably didn't want to build up your hopes.
THERESE	He was right to keep silent. We wouldn't dare to count on it.

She exchanges a glance with LAURENT.

LAURENT	Will you keep her occupied, monsieur? We must see to the wine.
MICHAUD	I shall delight in it.
LAURENT	The glasses, Thérèse.
THERESE	I'll get the best ones.

She goes off to the kitchen as MICHAUD *brings the stool closer to* MADAME RAQUIN *and sits.*

MICHAUD   We've been friends for a long while, you and I. You always did the talking before; now it's my turn. Watching's no good, madame, you've got to hurry up and get better, be a part of everything again. There's no-one to boss me about, these days! (*After studying her, he turns back to* LAURENT, *who is opening the wine.*) Something's wrong tonight. She's very black. I'll talk about the old days — that nearly always works.

LAURENT   She loved her life in Normandy. We were all going off there for a holiday, if this hadn't come about.

MICHAUD   (*back to* MADAME) What about when we first met — eh? I was only a young policeman then and you were the prettiest girl in Vernon. It was the year of the Gorge aux Loups murder, as I recall ... (THERESE *re-enters.*) Remember, madame? That woman and her lover, who murdered the husband?

THERESE *checks in her stride, but only momentarily. Then she takes the best glasses to* LAURENT *at the sideboard.*

He was a van-driver, wasn't he? And they tried to make it look like an accident. Soaked the old chap in absinthe and sent him over the cliff at Point Cabel. I talked it over with you at great length and I remember you saying whoever heard of a poor van-driver getting drunk on absinthe? So I went and searched their filthy cottage, found the bottles, and arrested them myself. (*He looks over at the lovers.*) My first big success. I got promotion and they both got the guillotine. (*A silence falls, during which the clock outside can be heard as it strikes.* MICHAUD *checks his large watch by it.*)

... six ... seven ... eight. He's late! By all that's wonderful, Grivet's going to be *late.*

GRIVET	(*appearing*) Oh no, he isn't. (*He comes up the stairs to join them.*)
	The shop bell's off the hook and I crept through the shop to surprise you. Good evening, Thérèse — Laurent.
LAURENT	(*nods*) Doctor
	Grivet crosses to place his umbrella in its usual position and to take off his goloshes.
GRIVET	Long faces? What's the matter with you all?
THERESE	Michaud's been raking over old bones.
GRIVET	Let me guess — the Wolf of Montmartre?
MICHAUD	Earlier that that.
GRIVET	The stranglings at Epinay? We haven't had that one for ages.
MICHAUD	Long ago and far away. Miles and miles away from Paris.
GRIVET	Then it must have been the van-driver in Vernon.
MICHAUD	Top marks. I can see my book's made a great impression on you.
GRIVET	He solved that within a week, you know. Murder usually takes him longer.
MICHAUD	But never as long as it's taking you to cure madame.
GRIVET	That's the difference between doctors and detectives. We can only work wonders, never miracles. Still, I can communicate with her, which is more than you can do.
MICHAUD	Then I wish you'd tell us what's wrong with her tonight. (*He moves away to light his pipe.*)
GRIVET	Certainly, certainly! One look, just one look, and I know exactly what's going on in that mind of hers.
MICHAUD	I can guess, of course. She thinks it's time we all had a drink.

LAURENT	(*apologetically*) It's your stories; they put it clean out of my head.

He goes to pour the wine as GRIVET *takes the place recently vacated by* MICHAUD *and turns on his best bedside manner.*

GRIVET	There now, let's have a nice, friendly little chat. Is there something you wish to say to us, apart from telling Michaud to mind his own business? (*Stares intently*) I've got it — she's hungry.
LAURENT	She had supper in her room before you came.

THERESE *is busy handing round the drinks.*

MICHAUD	A drink — perhaps that's what she needs.
GRIVET	I wouldn't advise it.
MICHAUD	Oh, not a whole glass, just a thimbleful. That couldn't harm, surely? And it makes her feel one of us, instead of — (*moves in towards her*)
GRIVET	(*not pleased*) Oh, very well. Just one sip — as long as someone else administers it. Laurent, you feed her as a rule, don't you?

LAURENT *offers his own glass to* MADAME RAQUIN'S *lips, but they are shut tight.*

LAURENT	She won't have it.
MICHAUD	I tell you, she's playing us up deliberately.
GRIVET	(*rises to him deprecatingly*) Michaud, you may have been the finest detective Paris ever had.
MICHAUD	(*gruffly*) I was a policeman, from beginning to end. Just a policeman. But we have a saying, doctor . . . you look, and you know. I looked at her tonight and I *know* she's trying to tell us something.
LAURENT	Thérèse, see if you can set his mind at rest.

THERESE *goes to her aunt and takes both of her hands, gazing deeply into her eyes.*

THERESE	(*at last*) She's perfectly happy, monsieur; she wants for nothing.

GRIVET	Well, now that's settled, can we get on with the game?
THERESE	Of course. Laurent, bring the dominoes.

LAURENT, pouring himself another drink at the sideboard, tries the top drawer.

LAURENT	I will if you'll unlock this drawer. (*To the others*) You didn't know the damn things were so precious, did you?
GRIVET	(*blinks*) Precious dominoes?
LAURENT	They must be. She keeps this drawer locked up all through the week.
THERESE	They're precious to me. They belonged to my husband.

An embarrassed pause, during which she unlocks the drawer and hands the box over to LAURENT.

LAURENT	I'm honoured. Does anyone mind if I take the holy chair as well?

Deliberately, he pushes CAMILLE'S armchair into its old position at the table, and sits in it.

THERESE	You've had too much to drink.
MICHAUD	But we've only just started!
THERESE	Laurent was out earlier in the day, seeing some old friends. You must excuse him.
LAURENT	They envy me, don't you, gentlemen? Now what was it Saint Camille used to say? (*Quotes*) 'Ladies and gentlemen — the pieces!' (*He cascades them on to the table.*) 'And may the best man win.' You'll notice he never included the ladies in that bit.
THERESE	(*flushing*) I never played. I shan't play now. (*She moves away.*)

All is now ready for the game, with MICHAUD, GRIVET and LAURENT at the table, and MADAME RAQUIN stationed next to LAURENT, who is shuffling the dominoes.

GRIVET	If you're going to smoke, I'd better have my usual cigar.
MICHAUD	Save your money, my friend, the pipe's gone out.
GRIVET	Oh. (*Determined*) Still . . . (*He takes his cigar-case out.*)
MICHAUD	What's more, I shan't light the thing again; not while I'm sitting next to madame.
GRIVET	(*takes his point*) That's most considerate. (*He coughs, and puts the case away.*)
	The three men take their dominoes and study them in dedicated silence. Suddenly —
THERESE	(*gasps*) Her hand —
	All look towards MADAME RAQUIN. *Her wizened index finger is curled like a brown claw over the table, and she is moving it slowly.*
MICHAUD	It's moving!
GRIVET	She's trying to write — it's a miracle. Madame's trying to write something on the table. Madame —
MICHAUD	Leave her alone. (*Watches, eagle-eyed*) I can't make that out.
GRIVET	It could have been an 'I' . . . or a 'T'
	LAURENT *rises slowly from his chair, his gaze fixed on the moving hand.*
MICHAUD	Here. (*He empties ash from his pipe on to the oilcloth table-cover.*)
	Write in the ash, madame — write in that.
	MADAME RAQUIN's *head is thrown back in anguish and she is sweating with effort, but the hand ploughs on.* LAURENT *moves involuntarily towards* THERESE.
LAURENT	Thérèse —
THERESE	Be quiet.
GRIVET	What's this, madame? You're your old self again. Just look at those fingers, dancing a proper little jig!

MICHAUD	Quiet, Grivet! She's made a capital 'T'.
GRIVET	Good heavens, so she has. 'T', that's it. She wants some tea.
MICHAUD	Nincompoop! Can't you read? She's written Thérèse's name. 'Thérèse and ...' go on, madame, go on.
GRIVET	'Thérèse and Laurent ...' Both your names.
MICHAUD	'Thérèse and Laurent have ... 'K' — (*As the hand pauses*) Well, what have they done?
GRIVET	It's no good, she's stopped.
MICHAUD	Rest a moment and then try again. Finish the sentence. Please, madame!

With a great effort of will, MADAME RAQUIN *brings her eyes round to look directly into* MICHAUD'S. *Her hand falls back in her lap.*

MICHAUD	She won't.
GRIVET	She can't, you mean.

He takes the hand and wipes it gently with his silk handkerchief, before carefully testing the fingers and the wrist.

LAURENT	Well?
GRIVET	Gone back to stone. I fear she will never move again.

THERESE *takes in a breath sharply as he folds* MADAME RAQUIN'S *hands in her lap.*

MICHAUD	If only she could have told us.
GRIVET	It may be as well she didn't; the strain was proving too much. Anyway, there's no mystery in what she meant, is there?
LAURENT	(*daring*) What do you think it was, doctor?
GRIVET	It's perfectly obvious. 'Thérèse and Laurent have kept me alive with their kindness.' That was it, I'm sure. 'My blessings on them both.' Something of that sort, almost certainly.

MICHAUD	And they'll have their just reward; here or hereafter.
	He turns to face the two of them and his face is grim.
LAURENT	That's an odd thing to say.
MICHAUD	It's rather an odd evening, monsieur, don't you agree?
THERESE	Go on. (*Pause*) Don't leave it at that.
MICHAUD	(*Shrugging*) All I'm saying is, the message couldn't have ended simply on kindness. We all know how much you've done for her.
GRIVET	And they're enjoying their reward this minute. Look at the two of them, with their arms entwined!
MICHAUD	Yes, I noticed.
GRIVET	It's so refreshing to see a couple so wrapped up in each other. And to think it's all thanks to me!
MICHAUD	(*heavily*) If I've told you once, I've told you a hundred times —
THERESE	(*embarrassed, breaking from* LAURENT) Please, gentlemen, I think she's had enough excitement for one evening.
GRIVET	Indubitably. (*Rises*) Michaud, our presence here is quite superflous. Where's my umbrella?
MICHAUD	(*rises, grumpily*) Where the hell do you think it is?
	He nods at the fireplace and GRIVET *crosses to get it, sitting to put on his goloshes first.*
GRIVET	Put her to bed, my dears; her pulse is racing.
	THERESE *brings* MICHAUD *his hat, but his eyes have gone back to* MADAME RAQUIN.
THERESE	Goodnight, monsieur.
MICHAUD	Was that all there was, old friend?
LAURENT	What do you think, Michaud? What do you really think?
MICHAUD	I think she changed her mind.

GRIVET	Nonsense. You saw her hand fall. You saw me examine it. She's spent, and there's an end of it.
MICHAUD	Perhaps; and perhaps not. Goodnight, everybody.
	He stumps off down the stairs.
GRIVET	Now what's come over him?
LAURENT	Goodnight, doctor. I'm sorry it was such a short evening.
GRIVET	There'll be others. Michaud, wait for me!
	He hurries out after his friend, his goloshes slopping awkwardly. LAURENT *waits till they have gone and then pulls the wheelchair round for* MADAME RAQUIN *to face him. He studies her intently.*
THERESE	It was a chance in a million.
LAURENT	It happened. What if it happens again?
THERESE	It can't. You heard what Grivet said.
	She goes off into the kitchen. LAURENT *starts to clear the dominoes away and then finds that* MICHAUD'S *pipe has been left on the table. He makes for the stairs with it to go out after the visitors but then changes his mind and sets the pipe aside.* THERESE *returns with a board on which is a small Vienna loaf and the kitchen knife. She puts them on the table.*
LAURENT	Another second and she'd have given us away.
THERESE	It's over and done with.
	She goes out again, now perfectly in control once more. LAURENT *picks up the knife and tests its sharpness against his thumb. He is about to cut bread then he feels the old lady's eyes upon him. He crosses round to her with the blade extended.* THERESE *returns with two plates and a bowl of salad.*
THERESE	Laurent — no!
LAURENT	So simple. Slash the wrists. They'd call it suicide.
THERESE	By someone who can't move?
LAURENT	She had the strength to write —

THERESE	But not to kill. Everything would come out. You know what that would mean.
	LAURENT *looks at her and then tosses the knife back on to the table.*
LAURENT	All right. But we'll never be safe again while she's alive.
THERESE	Eat something. You'll feel better.
LAURENT	I'll finish my wine.
	He throws the drink back and then fills up his glass once more. THERESE *sits to start her meal.*
THERESE	Stop dwelling on it, you'll only make things worse.
LAURENT	What am I supposed to do, ignore it? What if her speech came back? Michaud said that was the next step. Do you think she'd spare us then?
THERESE	It never will.
LAURENT	He'll find out, sooner or later. His mind was full of it when he left.
THERESE	If only you'd stop harping on Michaud!
LAURENT	Grivet, then. When I apologised for the evening, did you hear him? 'There'll be others' — what did he mean by that?
THERESE	Simply what he said. They know nothing. They're ordinary people, simple and uncomplicated.
LAURENT	They'll put us before a judge in the end. Think of that! Two clever murderers like us sent to the guillotine by a pair of simple, uncomplicated fools.
	THERESE *rises and moves about restlessly.*
THERESE	Oh God, let's talk about something else. Why does it always come back to this when we're left alone?
LAURENT	We're never alone. Perhaps she brings it back. Or you do.
THERESE	All I want is to escape from it.

LAURENT	We can never do that now.
THERESE	We must!
LAURENT	It's gone too far. It began the day you seduced me, here in this room. It'll go on until we pay for it. In full.
THERESE	Laurent, I don't want to fight with you. Can't you see I'm tired out? That I've had more than I can stand?
LAURENT	Go on, make a martyr of yourself as usual. That's all you're good for nowadays.
THERESE	Be careful.
LAURENT	Why? We died on each other long ago. (*Finishes his drink*)
THERESE	All right! We won't eat, we won't try to talk sensibly. You'll drink yourself into a rage and we'll finish up clawing each other's eyes out as usual.
LAURENT	People can't talk to each other when they're a million miles apart.
THERESE	I know why you turn like this every night. It suits you when we shout and rave at one another till you're exhausted. Then you can sleep.
LAURENT	You get no more sleep than I do.
THERESE	I dread the nights. If you knew what it was like, in that bedroom of hers. Like a tomb. I see Camille there all the time and sometimes wish to Heaven we'd never — never . . .

She breaks off and sinks her head in her arms.

LAURENT	Never killed him? That's what you were going to say, isn't it?
THERESE	You killed him. I didn't.
LAURENT	You were as much to blame as I was — more.
THERESE	No — no.
LAURENT	Lying there on that river-bank while he was asleep I whispered to you, told you what was in

my mind. Did you try and stop me? You got
into the boat with me, you let me do it.

THERESE   I was mad for you. I didn't realise what giving
way to you would mean.

LAURENT   Think back. I warned you when I was going to
overturn the boat. Did you stop me then? You
clung to me, and wished him dead.

THERESE   The two of us together, happy and in love. It
filled my mind. Even in the water.

LAURENT   Liar! You enjoyed the killing. You revelled in it.
Remember what happened on the way back in
the cab — we were on fire for each other.
That's what murder did for us, made
love-making all the better! You wanted him out
of your life.

THERESE   Not before he brought you here.

LAURENT   Two years ago. Look what those two years have
done to me. Was I like this when I first came
here? Drinking like a fish, afraid of my own
shadow? I was a decent human being but you
made me a murderer. All I can think of now is
the arrest, the trial and the guillotine. God help
me!

He sinks into CAMILLE'S *chair, his body shaking.*

THERESE   You'll give us both away. You'll be the one.

LAURENT   I don't care any more.

THERESE   Is this the brave Laurent? Is this the man who
wanted me so much he'd dare anything to have
me?

LAURENT   It's what you've made of him.

THERESE   And I once thought I loved you. If you want the
truth, I can't bear you near me. Every time I
see your hands, they're stained with Camille's
blood.

LAURENT   Camille — Camille — that's all I ever hear. It's
in every thought that comes out of your head.
It's in her eyes, every time she looks at me.

Camille did this, Camille did that. He was so
perfect, too perfect to be a saint! Poor Camille.
There was no living with him, now there's no
living without him.

THERESE   Laurent, for the last time —

LAURENT *leaps up wildly.*

LAURENT   Don't call me that! It's not my name. I'm not
Laurent any more, I'm turning into Camille. It
started with my hands. Now my voice, my face,
my brain! I *am* Camille. Soon I'll begin to
giggle and complain like him. Then, when I talk
like Camille, look like Camille, suffer like
Camille, maybe I'll have Camille's wife in my
bed again.

THERESE   Laurent — Camille — whoever you think you
are, all I know is I hate you.

LAURENT   Treacherous bitch! (*He strikes her full in the face
and knocks her to the ground. Immediately he is on his
knees beside her.*) I'm sorry ... sorry ... God
forgive me ... sorry.

She crawls away from him.

THERESE   He punishes me every day you walk the earth.

LAURENT   Not any more.

*He pulls himself to his feet and moves towards the
stairs.*

THERESE   (*fearfully*) Where are you going?

LAURENT   To give myself up. It's the only freedom I've
got left.

THERESE   (*defiantly*) Send them here then. I'll be waiting
I've faced everything better than you, all the
way through. I'll face the guillotine too.

She drags herself painfully upright, using CAMILLE'S
chair for leverage. LAURENT *stands stockstill, his back
to her.*

THERESE   Why don't you go? God damn you, *why don't
you go?*

Slowly he turns to face her. Tears stream silently down his face.

LAURENT   I can't. It's not for myself, all I want is peace. It's what they'd do to you, I can't *allow* that.

THERESE   (*wonderingly*) Laurent ...

LAURENT   I'll tell them I did it. That from beginning to end, you knew nothing about it.

Pause.

THERESE   After all I've said — you can do that for me?

LAURENT   Anything. Whatever you say, whatever you *are* ... I'll love you till I die.

He turns to go.

THERESE   Wait! (*She goes very close to him.*) I spoke madness just now. I was only testing your love. Believe it, my darling, it's you, it's always been you. Love me, that's our salvation. Hold me — love me now.

He crushes her in his arms and for a moment they gaze at each other, lost in a miraculous rediscovery. They are very near MADAME RAQUIN *and* THERESE'S *back is towards her. The old lady's hands come gradually into view. They clutch the knife. She plunges it deep into* THERESE *and then sinks back into her chair.* THERESE *slumps to the ground.*

LAURENT   Thérèse!

He goes down beside her and plucks the knife from her, then rises and backs in horror at the sight of her life's blood. MICHAUD'S *voice is heard on the stairs.*

MICHAUD   (*off*) May I come up? (*He comes into sight, breathless from hurrying.*) I was halfway home before I realised I'd forgotten my pipe — (*He turns into the room and pulls up short at what confronts him.*) Dear God in Heaven! (*Soundlessly, he crosses to the body and kneels to make a brief examination.*) Dead. (*He rises to face* LAURENT, *who still holds the knife, staring at him dully.*) You couldn't trust her then to keep your secret? that message tonight:

'Therese and Laurent have killed my son.' Guilt was written all over you both.

LAURENT   You think I could do this — to Thérèse?

MICHAUD   Who else, monsieur?

LAURENT *sways round to look at* MADAME RAQUIN, *who is once again immobile.*

A helpless invalid? She can't move hand or foot. Give me the knife.

LAURENT *gazes at him, broken. He passes the knife across and* MICHAUD *takes it in his gloved hand. Then he bends towards* MADAME RAQUIN.

MICHAUD   I'll send someone up, madame, you won't be alone long. (*To Laurent*) Come with me — now!

LAURENT *is taken off down the stairs at knife-point.* MADAME RAQUIN *stays absolutely motionless until they have gone and the house is quiet. Then she raises her head and looks directly at us. She is smiling a crooked smile.*

CURTAIN

PROPERTY PLOT

(Essentials)

ACT ONE, Scene 1

SET ONSTAGE	Coal scuttle with tongs and poker. Clock. Landscape picture above fire. Waste basket. Ashtray on table C. Box of dominoes in sideboard drawer. Cashbox with coins in second drawer. Corkscrew on sideboard. Spare glasses on sideboard. Empty wine bottle in sideboard cupboard. Embroidery basket on work-table or window-seat. Jacket (Laurent) on bed.
SET OFF R	Two bottles of champagne. Shop-bell on hook. Portrait of Camille, in sacking. Two ladder-back chairs, back to back. Bundle of wet clothing. Stage blood and small sponge. Medical bag with pills and stethoscope. Two bags of shopping. (French bread, etc.) Carpet bag with posy of flowers, box of cheroots, jar of coltsfoot jelly. Handsome bouquet of flowers. Bundle of nettles or thistles. Wedding posy (Thérèse). Bottle of vintage champagne. Wheelchair with cushions. Brown bag with three bottles of Chablis (corked).
SET OFF L.	Oil lamp. Four champagne glasses on tray. Cakes on cakestand. Four small plates. Tray with teapot, milk and sugar, tongs, strainer, four cups, saucers and spoons. Breadboard with hunks of bread and large

Kitchen knife.
Soup tureen and ladle.
Place mat.
Glass of water.
Vase ready for Thérèse's flowers.
Four good wine glasses.
Small Vienna loaf.
Two white plates.
Bowl of salad and server.

SET OFF
U.C. (*possibly
concealed in
alcove*)

Two worn dressing-gowns.
Robe (new, preferably white).
Tray with brush, comb, powder-box, white
ribbon, hairpins, hand-mirror, pin cushion.
Slippers.
Nightdress.

ACT ONE, Scene 2

STRIKE.

Used glasses.
Cakestand and cakes.
Used plates and tray.
All other used crockery and cutlery, etc.
Workbasket.
Landscape picture.
Sacking.
Spare ladder-back chairs.
Umbrella and goloshes.
Used ashtray.
Dominoes and box.

SET

Clean ashtray.
White tablecover.
Two soup dishes and spoons.
Vase of autumn flowers.

ACT TWO, Scene 1

STRIKE

Soup dishes and spoons.
Soup tureen and ladle.
White tablecover.

Discarded dressing-gown.
Empty wine bottle.

SET   Table in new position.
Chaise longue and Madame's armchair, ditto.
Stool, ditto.
Grivet's medical bag on table.

ACT TWO, Scene 2

STRIKE   Posy of flowers from mantelpiece.
Box of cheroots.
Jar of coltsfoot jelly.

SET   Bowl of roses on table.
White bedspread on bed.

ACT THREE

STRIKE   Nettles from waste basket.
Wedding posy.
Discarded clothing (Thérèse).
Bowl of roses from alcove.
Champagne bottle and used glasses.
Discarded clothing (Laurent).
Camille's portrait.
White bedspread.
Double bed from alcove.

SET   Landscape picture over fire.
Single truckle bed in alcove.
Crumpled bedclothes in a heap.
Clean ashtray on table.
Oilcloth cover on table.

PERSONAL PROPS

(Essentials)

CAMILLE   Four coins.

MME. RAQUIN Purse.
Walking stick.

GRIVET   Umbrella.
Goloshes.
Pince-nez.
Two silk handkerchieves.

	Cigar-case with four cigars. Watch and chain. Matches. Diary.
MICHAUD	Pipe. Pouch. Matches. Pocket-flask with screw-cap. Imposing watch and chain. Gloves.
LAURENT	Two cheroots. Matches.
THERESE	Lace handkerchief. Wedding ring. Chatelaine.

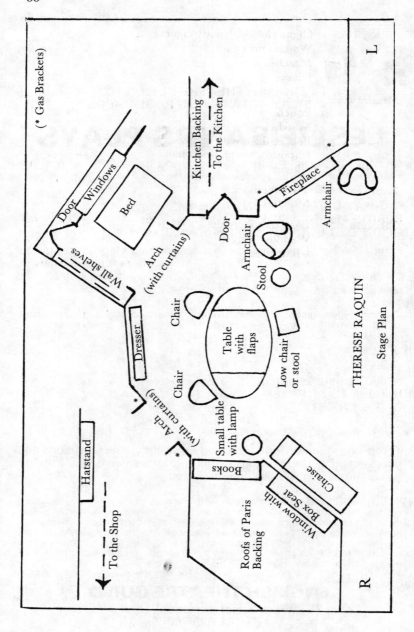

THERESE RAQUIN

Stage Plan

(* Gas Brackets)

L

R

To the Kitchen
Kitchen Backing
Fireplace
Armchair
Door
Armchair
Stool
Chair
Table with flaps
Low chair or stool
Chair
Dresser
Wall shelves
Arch (with curtains)
Bed
Windows
Door
Small table with lamp
Books
Arch (with curtains)
Hatstand
To the Shop
Roofs of Paris Backing
Window with Box Seat
Chaise